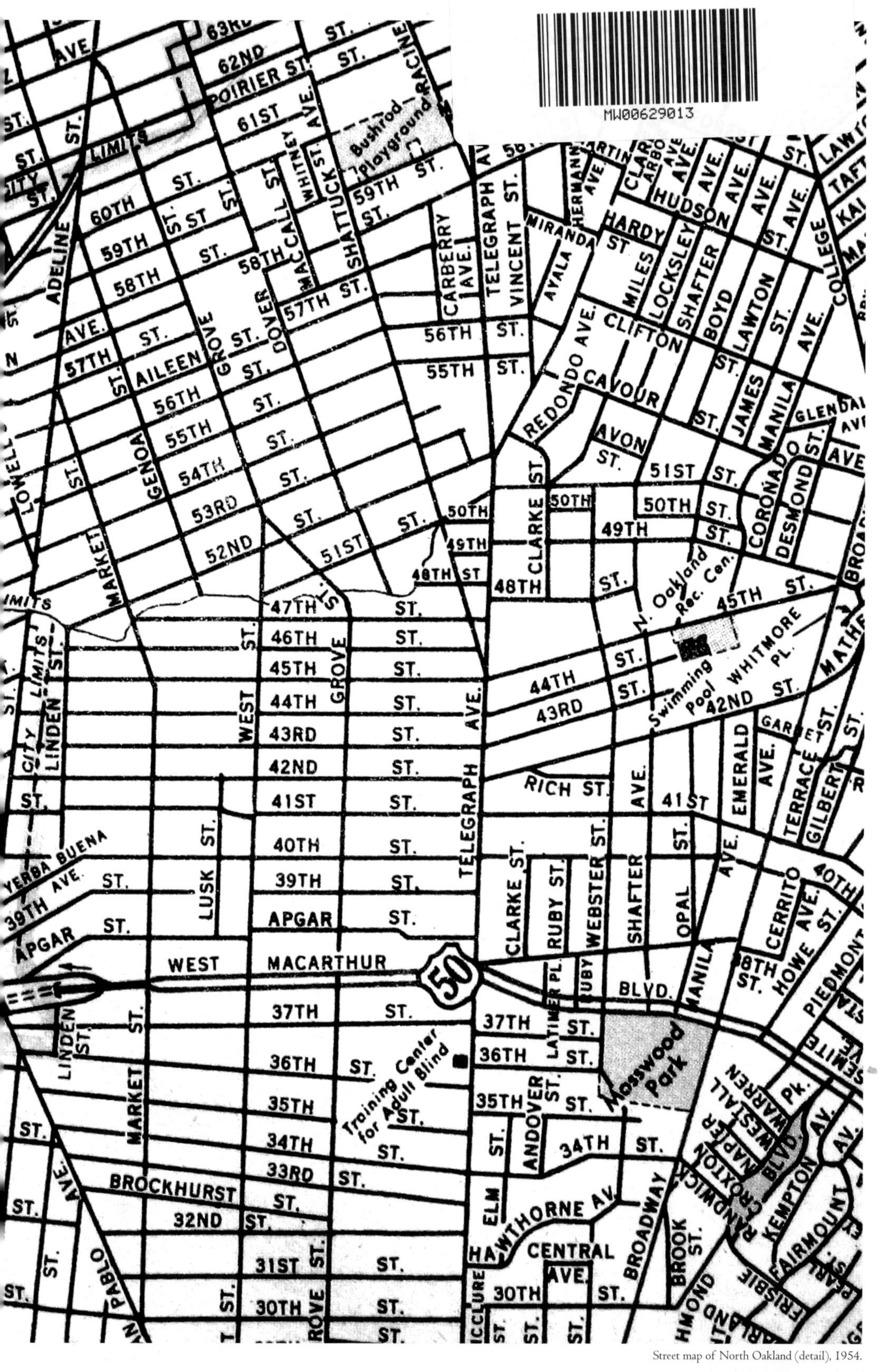

Street map of North Oakland (detail), 1954.

Temescal Legacies

Narratives of Change from a North Oakland Neighborhood

Studio One Art Center

Sacramento Northern Railway

Grove-Shafter Freeway

East Bay Negro Historical Society

Temescal Creek

JEFF NORMAN

SHARED GROUND

Published 2006 by Shared Ground
Printed in Canada on acid-free paper

Researched, written, and designed by Jeff Norman
Unless otherwise noted, all photographs in this book from 1997 to 2006 are by Jeff Norman.

ISBN: 0-9778893-0-0

10 9 8 7 6 5 4 3 2 1

SHARED GROUND
477 Rich Street, Oakland, CA 94609
(510) 653-7190
SharedGround@california.com
www.sharedground.org

Founded in 1997, SHARED GROUND is a community arts organization dedicated to enhancing the cultural and ecological vitality of the Temescal neighborhood of Oakland, California, and neighborhoods in general. Values underlying the projects of SHARED GROUND include sustainability, love of place, strengthening local identity, historic preservation, diversity, collaboration, and activism.

Front cover photographs: Les Paul, crew member, and Sacramento Northern train, Shafter near 41st Street (looking north), circa 1940, photo by Paul Smith; Grove-Shafter Freeway (looking eastward, 1974, courtesy of Department of Transportation. *Back cover photograph:* Tug of war, demonstration held on contested vacant lot, Cavour Street, early 1973, courtesy of Alphonse Durieux. *Photograph on overleaf of front page map:* 42nd Street overpass (looking west), 2005.

Funding for this book was generously provided by the Oakland City Council and the City of Oakland's Cultural Funding Program, and by the Alameda Countywide Clean Water Program.

The word "temescal," derived from the Aztec word for sweat lodge, was brought north from Mexico by the early Spanish colonists. Sweat lodges, often located near streams, were used by native peoples throughout the Americas for health and spiritual purposes. The legend is that Temescal Creek was named for a temescal that stood near its bank.

Contents

Lake Temescal stop (at north end of the lake), 1937. *Photo: Paul Smith*

4900 block of Telegraph Avenue, west side, 1941. *Courtesy of the Oakland History Room*

About This Book

The place we now know as the Temescal neighborhood of Oakland, California, has seen dramatic change over the past 150 years. Beginning in the 1860s when the village of Temescal first coalesced around Vicente Peralta's adobe and orchard near what is today the intersection of Telegraph and Claremont, to the town's growth and then annexation by the City of Oakland in 1897, to the influx to the Temescal neighborhood of refugees of the San Francisco earthquake and fire in 1906, and on through to the present, change in Temescal has been persistent.

This book explores five distinct developments in Temescal's more recent past, and the legacies they have left in the community. Corresponding to the book's five main sections, they include: 1) the joint effort in the late 1940s by the North Oakland community and the city's Recreation Department to purchase a former orphanage on 45th Street and convert it into the North Oakland Recreation Center and Studio One arts program; 2) the rise and fall of the Sacramento Northern Railway, an electric interurban train service that from 1913 to 1957 ran from its depot and rail yard at Shafter and 40th Street, up Shafter, through Oakland's Montclair district, and eventually all the way to Chico; 3) the development in the late 1950s and 1960s of the Grove-Shafter Freeway* through Temescal and Rockridge, and its impacts on the community; 4) the founding of the East Bay Negro Historical Society in the 1960s and the concurrent shifts in Temescal's demographics; and 5) the neighborhood battle in the early 1970s to prevent the county from undergrounding the four-block stretch of Temescal Creek from Hardy to Clarke streets.

Of Temescal's many historical developments worthy of attention, why these five? To begin with, as described in the following chapters, each of them had a profound physical or cultural impact on the neighborhood, and, directly or indirectly, each continues to shape our experience of Temescal today.

Secondly, despite the importance of these developments within Temescal's evolution, most Oaklanders are unfamiliar with them. Much if not all of the physical evidence of the Sacramento Northern Railway and Temescal Creek (notwithstanding the artificial stream near the Department of Motor Vehicles that many mistake for the

---

*The stretch of freeway that today makes up the combined Highway 24/I-980 west of the Caldecott Tunnel was known as the Grove-Shafter Freeway during its planning and construction, as well as for many years after. In this book, the freeway is identified according to the name in general use at the time being referenced.

actual creek) has long since vanished from the neighborhood. While a direct lineage exists, few can trace the connection between the East Bay Negro Historical Society from its early days on 45th and Grove Street* with today's distinguished African American Museum and Library at Oakland on 14th Street and Martin Luther King Jr. Way. Even in the cases of the Grove-Shafter Freeway and Studio One, for which obvious physical evidence exists, the freeway and art center are by now such long-standing features of the neighborhood landscape that we give little if any thought to how they came to be.

Thirdly, each of the five developments explored here provides an example of neighbors organizing to carry out a shared vision for the community. Sometimes, as when establishing a home for Studio One, all participants, including the city government, were aligned in the effort to create what everyone agreed was an important community asset. Often, neighbors have rallied *against* proposed "improvements," particularly when they seemed imposed from the outside. This was the case with both the building of the Grove-Shafter Freeway and the culverting of Temescal Creek, where political, institutional, and economic interests, often at a remove from North Oakland, threatened to undermine Temescal's traditional character by eliminating a cherished neighborhood feature. Sometimes the community's efforts resulted in extraordinary wins, sometimes not; but, as you will see, each of these stories illustrates how North Oaklanders, working together for the betterment of the neighborhood as a whole, have been instrumental in shaping Temescal's path as a community.

A final but equally important reason for the focus on these five aspects of the community's past relates to the primary way in which these stories are conveyed in *Temescal Legacies*—through personal reminiscences. At the heart of each of the five chapters are edited interviews, conducted in 2004 and 2005, with persons who were directly involved in the events described. Most of them—some now in their eighties or nineties—were long-time Oakland residents, while others lived in the neighborhood for a briefer time but at a moment when key events were unfolding. Having first been identified and then successfully tracked down (several no longer live in the Bay Area), each of these men and women expressed an immediately willingness to be interviewed. Now, thanks to their generosity in sharing their recollections, their voices have become part of the neighborhood's historical record. While their accounts—often conveying strong viewpoints—might not cover every aspect of the topic or be entirely free of the

---

* Grove Street is the former name of Martin Luther King Jr. Way. The street was renamed in honor of the civil rights leader by the City of Berkeley in 1985 and by the City of Oakland shortly thereafter. In this book, the street is identified according to the name in use at the time being referenced.

Organizers at a demonstration to save Temescal Creek and establish a park on Cavour Street, early 1973. *Photo: Alphonse Durieux*

inconsistencies of memory, they offer valuable insights that are unavailable elsewhere. They also make for compelling stories about the neighborhood.

Interwoven with these first-person narratives and fleshing out the events, places, and people described in the interviews are photographs, maps, and excerpts of published accounts from the time. Of the almost 250 photographs included (most of which are previously unpublished), many—especially the "then and now" pairings of images—show how the neighborhood has physically changed over time. The intent in combining these different kinds of visual and written elements has been to create an artful array of information that is lucid and aesthetically rewarding while also suggestive of larger, open-ended questions about Temescal's evolving identity.

Although each chapter focuses on a particular aspect of change in Temescal's evolution, these were not discrete events or processes but were all interconnected. The Sacramento Northern Railway (created in part to transport people from one side of the Oakland Hills to the other and to spur real estate development along its route) eventually succumbed to the growing use of the automobile; the ascendancy of the automobile was a major incentive for the building of the Grove-Shafter Freeway (also created to transport people through the hills and to spur development in Contra Costa County). Building the freeway depressed property values along its route through Temescal, allowing the East Bay Negro Historical Society to set itself up in an inexpensive storefront on Grove Street. Putting in the freeway caused Temescal Creek to flood more frequently, which in turn led the county to bury the creek in a culvert. With each successive chapter of *Temescal Legacies,* these and other connections become more evident.

40th Street, just east of Grove (looking west), 1939. *Photo: Ted Wurm*

In a sense, the chapters are also linked through those who witnessed and participated in these events. As mentioned, the persons interviewed for *Temescal Legacies* were chosen because of their experiences pertaining to one of the book's five chapter topics. However, many of them had memories that were relevant to other chapters as well. When we consider that the community-shaping events described in this book all took place within the small, shared arena of the neighborhood and within a relatively short period of time, it stands to reason that those interviewed (like many of their neighbors at the time) would have had some knowledge of each of these issues. As a result, the interviewees proved even more valuable as resources than originally thought—and why several of them are heard from in more than one chapter.

While the book's focus is on changes that occurred in Temescal, these events also reverberated beyond the neighborhood. Thus, for decades following the removal of the Sacramento Northern on Shafter Avenue, public debate continued over whether the portion of the railroad right-of-way that climbed through Shepherd Canyon above Oakland's Montclair district should be turned into a super highway to Contra Costa County, preserved as a mass transit route through the hills, sold off to private developers, or turned into public open space (a combination of the latter two prevailed). The hundreds of families whose homes in Temescal and Rockridge were demolished to build the Grove-Shafter Freeway moved elsewhere—often to the other side of the Caldecott Tunnel (from where, like thousands of other new suburbanites, they now regarded the new freeway as a godsend). Studio One's unique, affordable art classes drew patrons and instructors from throughout the Bay Area. Building the Grove-Shafter

40th Street, just east of Martin Luther King Jr. Way (looking west), 2005.

Freeway and culverting Temescal Creek increased the amount of sediment and toxins pouring into San Francisco Bay. Turning the lens around, these developments in Temescal also reflected major technological, sociological, and environmental shifts in the larger society. In communities across America, where automobiles and freeways have replaced streetcars and railways, where land has been ever more intensely developed and nature increasingly paved over, where historically disadvantaged citizens have fought for recognition and equal access to housing and employment, similar stories can be told.

The aspects of Temescal's evolution addressed in the book make up only a small part of the neighborhood's intricate history, and even those explored here deserve further attention. Still, the hope is that in offering a glimpse of some of the ways in which Temescal has changed, this book will help increase our understanding and appreciation of the neighborhood, and thus our connection to it.

In the way that squarely looking at a problem can be a first step toward solving it, this book is also an attempt to acknowledge the spiritual dislocation—the loss of sense-of-place—that the Temescal community has struggled with during the past forty-five years, as society-wide trends, local demographic shifts, and land use decisions by government agencies have saddled the neighborhood with a multitude of challenges. Given the ever accelerating change that is now a feature of every American urban place—including, locally, the surge in the housing market and the recent trend toward higher density residential development along Temescal's commercial corridors—a crucial question is: How do we rebuild a sustainable, culturally vital and diverse neighborhood, where housing is affordable, public transit is a viable option, the natural world is experienced more intimately, we can walk to a thriving business district, our public schools flourish, our streets are safe, and community participation is robust? In addition to reminding ourselves of all the things that we love about Temescal and that are important to preserve, taking a look at what has worked in the past and where society's and our local community's blindspots have been is a good place to start.

It is also useful to remember, as the stories in *Temescal Legacies* illustrate, that neighbors working together and inspired by community values is a long Temescal tradition—one worth celebrating and building upon. ✦

Jeff Norman
June 2006

A Note on Temescal's Boundaries

Temescal's boundaries, never officially fixed, have always been open to interpretation—and in flux. This book, which is about change in Temescal, would therefore be incomplete if it did not include some discussion of the neighborhood's changing borders. In truth, this theme flows throughout the book like an undercurrent, linked as it is to the many physical and social changes that *Temescal Legacies* explores (maps of the neighborhood, pre- and post-freeways, have been provided at the beginning and end of the book). To set this discussion in motion, following is a brief summary of some of the ways in which the neighborhood's geographical identity has shifted over time.

In the latter half of the 19th Century, as an unincorporated town in Alameda County, Temescal was generally considered to be everything north of the Oakland city limit at 36th Street to the Berkeley border, and from Broadway/College west to the Emeryville line. Even after annexation by the City of Oakland in 1897 and through the 1920s,

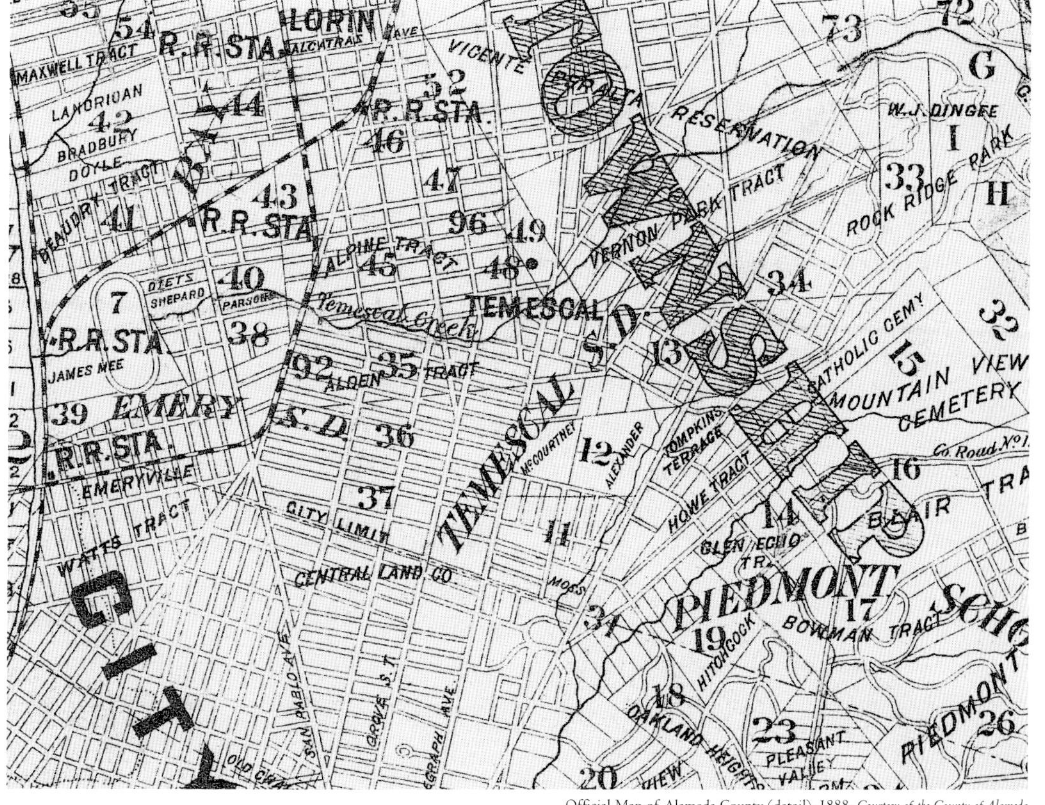

Official Map of Alameda County (detail), 1888. *Courtesy of the County of Alameda*

this definition remained largely intact, as we learn in the chapter on the Grove-Shafter Freeway from Raymond Mellana, who grew up on Grove and 46th Street.

By the 1940s, as Ray Raineri describes later in the book, his family home on Market Street, three blocks west of Grove, was considered to be just outside of Temescal in what his relatives and neighbors referred to, simply, as North Oakland. That the area west of Grove no longer was perceived by many as falling within Temescal might have been due in part to the commercial corridor along Grove that had developed independently of Temescal's business district on Telegraph Avenue.

Grove and 55th Street (looking northeasterly), 1944. *Courtesy of the Oakland History Room*

However, as Madison Harvey and Gladys Jordan suggest in the chapter on the East Bay Negro Historical Society, there were additional factors. For them and many other African Americans, Grove Street well into the 1950s also marked the edge of a world east of which they rarely if ever ventured. So entrenched had Grove become as a racial barrier, reinforced by years of institutional redlining and other racially discriminatory practices that made it nearly impossible for African Americans to purchase homes and establish businesses east of Telegraph, that many like Madison and Gladys didn't know that a distinct neighborhood called Temescal lay just beyond their own. The building of the Grove-Shafter Freeway in the 1960s, whose route some claimed was chosen to reinforce Grove Street as a racial divide, only further solidified Temescal's western boundary—even as legal, social, and economic factors enabled more and more African Americans, drawn by Temescal's affordable, well maintained bungalows, to cross over the line for the first time.

The Grove-Shafter Freeway redefined Temescal's northern edge as well. For many, including the Temescal Merchants Association whose purview traditionally has extended along Telegraph Avenue from 40th Street to 56th Street, Temescal's northern boundary was literally set in concrete by the freeway where it curves to the east toward Rockridge and crosses Telegraph just above 55th Street. Meanwhile, other neighbors and local community groups have come to regard 51st Street as Temescal's northern boundary. How do we account for this apparent discrepancy? Once again, we can look to the Grove-Shafter Freeway, when in the early 1970s, 51st Street was transformed from a small, residential side street into a significantly widened feeder route to the new freeway. Ever since, the fast-paced 51st Street has functioned

Construction of the Grove-Shafter Freeway and MacArthur Freeway (I-580) interchange, 1968. *Courtesy of Department of Tranportation*

as a physical and psychological boundary, having split off from Temescal an area that is now considered part of lower Rockridge (a term probably first introduced by local realtors).

For many, 40th Street, built extra wide over a century ago to accommodate Key System streetcars, came to replace 36th Street as Temescal's southern boundary. Meanwhile, Broadway, which was significantly busier when it served as a major access route to the tunnel through the hills prior to the opening of the Grove-Shafter Freeway, has consistently defined Temescal's eastern edge.

While the more recent reconfigurations of the local landscape—the Grove-Shafter Freeway and the widening of 51st Street—have changed the way many North Oaklanders define Temescal geographically, older, traditional definitions have not completely died out. For instance, many residents west of Highway 24, and some south of 40th Street, continue to identify with Temescal (sometimes feeling forsaken by it). The ambiguity of Temescal's borders manifests in other ways as well: witness the tendency of some North Oakland realtors to apply the term "lower Rockridge" to the neighborhood *south* of 51st Street (a trend that should also serve to remind us that *how* Temescal is defined has always partly depended on *who* is doing the defining).

40th Street, at Opal (looking west), showing Key System C Line train (center) and the Sacramento Northern yard (on right), 1953. *Courtesy of John Harder*

For all these reasons, and in the absence of any legal definition (census tracts and police beats aside), it is not surprising that, for many, Temescal's boundaries remain unclear. This can leave us with a feeling that contradicts an almost built-in need to know what constitutes our "home turf"—the place, beyond our actual residence, that is most familiar to us.

After reading this book and with a better understanding of how Temescal's boundaries have changed over time, it might be possible to think of the neighborhood not as a single, fixed entity but as an assortment of areas, one superimposed over the other, with semi-permeable edges, each slightly different, all valid. Or, maybe Temescal's boundaries are best left to each of us to define by examining our own subjective experience of when we feel we are entering and leaving our home turf. One way or another, when we say we live in Temescal, some part of us wants to be sure of what we mean. Perhaps this is because to know the answer is another way to know ourselves. ✦

Ladies' Relief Society's Home for Aged Women (looking west), with the intersection of 42nd Street and Opal at left, 1917.
Photo: Harry Courtright. Courtesy of the Oakland Museum of California

Junior Theater, Studio One, 1960. *Courtesy of Eileen Suzio*

Studio One

The Confluence of Community and City

Studio One, 1999. *Photo: David Meiland*

Introduction

Although the Studio One Art Center at 365-45th Street has operated in the Temescal neighborhood for over five decades, in recent years this unique, city-run facility dedicated to fostering the creative spirit has been one of Oakland's best kept secrets. That, however, was not the case back in 1947 when the North Oakland Area Council launched an extensive fundraising drive to purchase the building. Their goal in acquiring the property was to donate it to the city for use as a recreation center, and just about everybody in North Oakland—residents, businesses, school children, union members, and social clubs—knew it.

Many no doubt also knew the building in its earlier days when it served as an orphanage. For decades it had shared a ten-acre parcel that extended from 42nd to 45th streets with a home for elderly women (what became known as the Matilda Brown Home, on 42nd Street) and another for infants—all owned and operated by the Ladies' Relief Society of Oakland. Inspired by the great Chicago fire in 1871, the Society formed in 1872 (making it one of California's oldest charities) to help Oakland's indigent women and children. The organization built the two-story, brick and shingle, U-shaped children's home in 1894. A fire in 1906 destroyed the second story, but the facility was quickly rebuilt. Boys and girls, either orphaned or from families too poor to provide for them, continued to live there through the 1930s, after which child welfare programs shifted away from institutionalization to a foster care model.

Children's home, now Studio One, showing 45th Street at upper right; nursery, now Park Day School, at middle left; and home for aged women (demolished), lower left, circa 1920. *Courtesy of the Oakland Museum of California*

During World War II, the Ladies' Relief Society leased the building to the Army. In 1947, when the North Oakland Area Council became interested in purchasing the former children's home and what had been the boys' playground on the west side of the building, the Ladies' Relief Society was ready to sell.

That the building became the North Oakland Recreation Center and home to the infant Studio One program was the result of a remarkable confluence of factors. A local $600,000 bond measure, approved by voters in 1945, funded the construction of five municipal pools throughout the city. Oakland Technical High School, the immediate neighbor to the east of the Ladies' Relief Society property, was in line for one of the pools, and the former boys' playground offered a perfect place to build it.

Another crucial factor was the North Oakland community's post-war determination to establish a recreation center in Temescal. From the interview with Aldo Guidotti, which follows, we glimpse a Temescal that in the 1940s was significantly different from today. As the East Bay's "Little Italy," where residents of northern Italian heritage far outnumbered those of Irish, German, and Scandinavian descent, Temescal was a relatively homogeneous, tightly knit, extensive network of neighbors, merchants, organizations, schools, and social clubs. (The impressive number of active local organizations is evident from the donor list, beginning on page 22.) Add to this the right blend of leadership and the high degree of civic-mindedness that prevailed at the time, and we begin to understand how remarkable the achievement was of collecting donations—one by one—to purchase what was in 1947 dollars an expensive piece of real estate.

Once the community secured title to the building on 45th Street, what enabled Studio One to take root there was the Oakland Recreation Department's sense of mission in meeting the needs of the community. As we learn from the interview with Carol Pulcifer, the Recreation Department's unique history and philosophy were essential in first supporting the controversial idea of a city-run arts program for youth *and* adults, and then ensuring a home for it at the North Oakland Recreation Center. The department went on to build a staff that at all levels believed in the Studio and continued to fight for the precious city resources the program needed to flourish. In time Studio One went from being a North Oakland program to a city-wide institution.

Adult jewelry class, Studio One, 1954. *Courtesy of the Oakland History Room*

In May of 2005, after over half a century of offering art and theater classes to adults, youth, and families from throughout Oakland and beyond—and after years of deferred maintenance, Studio One closed its doors to prepare for a $12.5 million renovation and seismic retrofit. Echoing the community effort in 1947 to purchase the building, an active group of Studio One supporters fought to ensure that funding for the building's renovation was included in a city bond measure and then worked tirelessly towards its passage in November 2002. When it opens its doors (planned for summer, 2007), Studio One, a completely renovated studio arts facility, is sure to be Oakland's best kept secret no more.

Deed

RECREATION CENTER COMMITTEE OF THE NORTH OAKLAND AREA COUNCIL,

a non-profit corporation, -

- , the first part y , hereby

Grants to the City of Oakland, a municipal corporation, the second party, all that real property situated in the City of Oakland, County of Alameda, State of California, described as follows:

Beginning at the point of intersection of the southern line of 45th Street with the western boundary line of that certain parcel of land described in deed from Ladies' Relief Society, a corporation, to City of Oakland, a municipal corporation, dated April 19, 1923 and recorded April 26, 1923 in Book 412 of Official Records, at page 293, in the office of the Recorder of Alameda County, California: and running thence along the said line of 45th Street, North 87 degrees, 03 minutes West (the bearing of said line of 45th Street being taken as North 87 degrees, 03 minutes West for the purpose of this description) 315.50 feet, to the eastern boundary line of the "Shafter Avenue Tract, Oakland, California," filed February 13, 1907 in Map Book No. 22, at page 33, in the office of said Recorder; thence, leaving said line of 45th Street and along the eastern boundary line of said tract, South 10 degrees, 19 minutes West 260.65 feet to the southern line of 44th Street as shown upon said map; thence, leaving said boundary line of the above mentioned "Shafter Avenue Tract", South 87 degrees, 03 minutes East 324.87 feet to a point on the western boundary line of the hereinabove mentioned parcel of land deeded to the City of Oakland; thence along last said boundary line North 0 degrees, 28 minutes East 26.32 feet, South 87 degrees, 03 minutes East 22.45 feet, and North 2 degrees, 57 minutes East 232.23 feet to the point of beginning.

Being a portion of Plot No. 12, "Kellersberger's Map of the Ranchos V. & D. Peralta" filed January 21, 1857 in Map Book No. 17, at page 12, in the office of said Recorder.

SUBJECT, however, to a right-of-way along the southern boundary of the above described property in favor of the Ladies Relief Society Of Oakland, a benevolent corporation, the nature, terms and conditions of said right-of-way being more particularly described and expressed in that certain deed dated October 25, 1947, from the Ladies Relief Society Of Oakland, a benevolent corporation, as Grantor, to the Recreation Center Committee Of The North Oakland Area Council, a non-profit corporation, as Grantee, which said deed was recorded in the Office of the County Recorder of Alameda County on October 31, 1947, in Book No. _____, at page ______.

THIS DEED is made subject to the covenants and conditions herein contained:

(1) That the above-described property shall always be used as a public recreation center for the benefit of the residents of the City of Oakland;

(2) That prior to the first day of January, 1949, the Grantee shall commence construction of a public swimming pool on a portion of the above-described property; and

(3) That prior to the first day of January, 1949, the existing two-story building situated on the property shall have been renovated by the Grantee and made available for use by the residents of the City of Oakland.

PROVIDING, however, that a breach of any of the foregoing conditions shall cause said above-described property to revert to the said Grantor, who shall have the right of immediate re-entry upon said property in the event of any such breach.

IT IS FURTHER understood and agreed that the stipulations, agreements and conditions herein contained are to apply to and bind the successors and assigns of the respective parties hereto.

IN WITNESS WHEREOF, said corporation has executed these presents by its officers thereunto duly authorized, this 26th day of January, 1948.

RECREATION CENTER COMMITTEE OF THE
NORTH OAKLAND AREA COUNCIL,
a non-profit corporation

by Aldo P. Giudotti, Chairman

by Emmet Giusto, Treasurer

Aldo Guidotti

In 1946, when Aldo Guidotti opened his law office at 4918 Telegraph, he was the only practicing attorney in Temescal. Twenty-six years old and a graduate of UC Berkeley's Boalt Hall, Aldo moved into a small office above Pete Tira's furniture store (where the Temescal Cafe is today) and into a neighborhood where he did not know another living soul. In those early days, his clients were mostly retirees, "old-timers whose dollars were sitting edgewise. They'd come up to me for advice and I was lucky to get two dollars."

A practical man with a lot of time on his hands and with a community-minded bent, Aldo threw himself into several local service organizations. In a very short time he was at the center of a North Oakland community fundraising campaign to purchase and donate to the Cty of Oakland the property on 45th Street that today is home to the Studio One Art Center and Temescal Pool.

In 1960, Aldo and his partner, Ray Mellana, moved their law office from Telegraph Avenue to 4895 Shattuck (demolished in 2005), upstairs from which Aldo, his wife, Bernadine, and their young daughter had been living since the early 1950s. Although Aldo and his family moved to Orinda a few years later, he maintained the Shattuck Avenue office until 1989, when he moved his practice to Orinda. Aldo, who still practices law, has served the Orinda community as both city councilmember and mayor.

The Whole Temescal Area was Active

When I first moved to Temescal to open my law office in January 1946, Temescal was like a small village. We had the Roma Restaurant at 51st and Telegraph, which was equivalent to what you find in North Beach. People from downtown would meet there for lunch. There was McDonnell Florist and Nursery, on the east side of Claremont Avenue, right where it comes into Telegraph. We had the Genova Deli—in its old location—which was always full of customers. Fiorio Hardware had been on the southwest corner of Telegraph and 48th Street since the 1920s. The Question Mark bar was across 48th Street. Across Telegraph, on the corner of 48th Street, was a grocery store, and next to that, going north, was the Temescal Pharmacy. Then came Len and Bud's bar, which ran an excellent Chinese

Telegraph Avenue and 48th Street (looking north), 1947. *Courtesy of Ray Raineri*

restaurant. Next door was Breschi's Department Store, which had been there for a long time. The Barrell House was on 51st and Telegraph, and Brause's, which all the college kids knew, was at 56th. The old, famous Emil Villa's was at 45th—I remember when he opened in the 1940s. The whole Temescal area was active.

We also had a northern police station on 52nd Street, just west of Telegraph. (In those days, Oakland had an eastern police station as well.) It worked effectively for police protection, because the officers got to know the community, and they stayed. The captain, Dave Minney, was very active in local affairs.

When I came to Temescal, I didn't know a single person. My landlord was Pete Tira, one of the two men who had started Genova's. My office was above Pete's furniture store—where the cafe is today. I subsequently found out that he had been hunting pheasants up at my family's ranch in Orland, where I grew up. From my office I could look across the street and right into the old Genova deli.

Soon after I opened my office, I became active in the Temescal Merchants Association. The area represented by the Association extended from about 40th Street up to 56th, and from Broadway to this side of Grove Street—Grove had its own business area. Of course, that was before the freeway went in. The North Oakland Optimist Club, which we formed in 1947, had more than 75 members at its peak. I was president of both organizations in 1948. I incorporated the Temescal Merchants Association (which had been around since 1917), the North Oakland Optimists, and a half-dozen other clubs. I'd usually do this as charitable work.

The Opportunity

The idea for the North Oakland Recreation Center all started in early 1947 when the school district needed a site for a swimming pool for Oakland Technical High School. The opportunity came up to acquire an adjacent two-acre site on 45th Street from the Ladies' Relief Society for around $27,000. There was a large, older building on the property that originally had been built by the Society as an orphanage. It needed some attention, but it was a sizable parcel of land, and next to the building was ample room to put in a swimming pool.

Children's Home, circa 1898. The front originally faced south toward the other buildings on the Ladies' Relief Society property. *Courtesy of the Oakland History Room*

Studio One Art Center, 365-45th Street (looking south), 2005.

The concept for the North Oakland Recreation Center came about in large part because of the availability of that building. Our goal was to raise funds to purchase the property and deed it over to the city for it to be used specifically for recreational purposes. We wanted children to have a place where they could have some activities and programs. With the schools nearby, we felt this would be both a good use for the property and of benefit to the public.

The North Oakland Area Council, which took in a broader scope of community-related activities, had been formed around that time. In October of 1947, we established a Recreation Center Committee of the North Oakland Area Council specifically for the acquisition and donation to the city of the Ladies' Relief Society property. I did the legal work necessary to form the committee as a non-profit corporation so that donations could be tax-deductible. I also served as the committee's chairman.

We had an option to purchase the property that had a time limit on it. There was a real estate broker involved who had gotten the option. We were able to get it from him, but we had to pay something to do it.

A 22-room building which has served as an orphanage and headquarters for a military police unit of the U.S. Army will become a part of one of the most complete social and recreation facilities in Oakland if plans of the North Oakland Area Council materialize.

The building is now part of the property of the Ladies' Relief Society and is located on 45th Street behind Technical High School. Included in the section the council hopes to purchase and turn over to the city is 1-1/2 acres of wooded land.

Should the building and grounds be purchased, the city plans to build one of the five pools authorized by the electorate on one section.

Oakland Tribune
June 29, 1947

We Had a Lot of Support

As part of the effort to raise money, we undertook a program of selling little "one foot" certificates for fifty cents. We took small donations, naturally—a dollar, five, ten—whatever we could get. This was right after World War II and the economy wasn't all that great. To put it in perspective, when I opened my law office in Temescal, the rent was $65 a month. Recreation wasn't foremost in people's minds—surviving, making a living was. But we knew that if we waited to do this until the economy was great, the price of property would be prohibitive—so we'd be faced with a similar problem.

In those years, we had our annual fall parade down Telegraph—we still had the streetcar tracks then! Previously it had been known as the Halloween Parade, but we changed it to the Children's Day Parade to avoid the vandalism that sometimes accompanies Halloween. It was quite a parade, with a lot of participation. The Police Department's motorcycle squad led the way with their sirens going. That got everybody excited. The Children's Day Parades were two- and three-day affairs. That's why they took so much time to organize. They helped us raise money, though, both through donations and by being able to get the word out about our fundraising effort. All of the money raised from the parades in 1947 and 1948 was put into a fund to acquire the Ladies Relief Society property.

Raising the money took some real doing. We had all these various clubs in Temescal, and I belonged to a lot of them, as you do when you're a young lawyer trying to get business. I was interested in the recreation center project, but I also participated because it was a way of getting known in the community. It required an awful lot of time, of course, but starting a small law practice, I had the time. It's like so many organizations: once you get involved, you've got to have the time to devote to it.

We had a lot of support from all of the local organizations—the Temescal Merchants Association, Optimist Club, Temescal Sportsmens Club, an Order of the Moose, the Columbo, Liberty and Fratellanza clubs—all Italian clubs, and the North Central YMCA. The Oakland Scavengers were involved; even though they no longer were strictly a North Oakland company, the owners had all come from Temescal. The East Bay Machinists Union, which was city-wide, was in-

TOKEN

Deed of Gift

TO THE

Children of Oakland

This is to certify Aldo P. Guidotti

has purchased and deeded to the City of Oakland, 100 square feet of land for the exclusive use as a

Recreation Center

IN

North Oakland

DATED Jul 1 1947.

4900 Telegraph Avenue
Oakland 9, California

Member North Oakland Recreation Center Committee

Courtesy of Aldo Guidotti

Bellini's Restaurant, 4126 Telegraph (looking south), circa 1967. *Courtesy of the Oakland Cultural Heritage Survey*

volved, and all of the public schools in North Oakland raised funds.

A lot of the same people in the Optimist Club belonged to the Temescal Merchants Association. The merchants were very active—we had over 100 members back then. It was quite a little business district. There was a little paper called the *Oakland Telegraph*, which was another way we let the public know about the fund drive. I wrote an article for the paper outlining what the project involved and the history of the Recreation Center Committee and the North Oakland Area Council.

We had fundraising dinners at Bellini's, on Telegraph above 41st, which had a big back room. The Optimist Club, I believe, sponsored a raffle and dinner at the old Liberty Club hall, which used to be at 44th and Adeline. We sold a lot of tickets. We gave away TVs and other prizes—all from North Oakland businesses. Either they were donated, or we bought them. A lot of the businesses in Temescal helped out.

Captain Dave Minney from the northern police station was on the Recreation Center Committee. Although they were paid city employees, the director of the Recreation Department as well as other staff were also active in the work we were doing. Aleen Graves in particular was very involved. Even though Oakland had almost as many people in it as it has today, it was run by the Oakland city manager—Jack Hassler. You could talk to him and get things done without having to go through a half dozen chains of command.

With all the participation and activities—programs and raffles—the project became known. We started getting some real donations. The Oakland Scavengers gave $1,000, which was a really big sum in those days. The Grove Street Merchants gave even more. Our Optimist Club donated $1,000. The East Bay Machinists Union was another large contributor.

It took over a year to raise all the money. At the end we were a few thousand dollars shy, which the city chipped in to complete the deal. We didn't receive title until we paid for it in full. When we got it, we deeded it to the city. But we put in a provision whereby the property would come back to the Recreation Center Committee if the city failed to use it for recreational purposes for the citizens of Oakland.

Directors of the City Recreation Board have authorized [city Superintendent of Recreation, Robert] Crawford to work with the Public Buildings and Electrical departments on plans for remodeling the structure. . .

City Manager John F. Hassler has approved the board's proposal to develop the structure for use as a recreational center.

It is also planned to house the costume division of the department on the lower floor of one of the wings. The thousands of costumes owned by the city are now stored in Mosswood Park.

Oakland Tribune
August 26, 1948

Background: Telegraph Avenue, 4900 block, west side, 1941. *Courtesy of the Oakland History Room*

This recreation building and the two-acre parcel of land, including the site of the Temescal Pool, was acquired on October 21, 1947, for the total sum of $27,500.00 by the Recreation Committee of the North Oakland Area Council, a non-profit corporation, through voluntary contributions on the basis of 50¢ for each square foot from the following public spirited organizations and individuals named hereon, among others.*

City of Oakland
13,000 sq. ft.

Technical High School
3,150 sq. ft.

Grove Street Merchants
3,050 sq. ft.

E. H. Vernon
2,000 sq. ft.

East Bay Automotive
Machinist Lodge #1546
I. A. of W.
2,000 sq. ft.

Oakland Scavenger Co.
2,000 sq. ft.

Aahmes Shrine Circus
1,000 sq. ft.

Tiny Heller
1,000 sq. ft.

North Oakland Optimist Club
1,000 sq. ft.

Temescal Merchants Assn.
800 sq. ft.

Golden Gate P.T.A.
550 sq. ft.

Bartenders Local #52
500 sq. ft.

Oakland Lodge B.P.O.E.
500 sq. ft.

Oakland Round Table
500 sq. ft.

Columbo Club
400 sq. ft.

Fratellanza Club
400 sq. ft.

Liberty Club
400 sq. ft.

Ligure Club
400 sq. ft.

Milk Wagon Drivers
Union Local 302
400 sq. ft.

North Oakland Kiwanis Club
400 sq. ft.

Business & Professional
Women's Club
300 sq. ft.

ICE Wagon Drivers Local 610
200 sq. ft.

Al Wascher
200 sq. ft.

Kiwanis Club of Emeryville
200 sq. ft.

West of Market Boys
200 sq. ft.

L. D. MacGregor
200 sq. ft.

Women League
Plymouth Church
200 sq. ft.

John McDonnell
200 sq. ft.

Woodrow Wilson Jr. High
200 sq. ft.

James J. Nolan
200 sq. ft.

Frank J. Youell
200 sq. ft.

Oakland Moose Lodge
200 sq. ft.

Woodrow Wilson P.T.A.
200 sq. ft.

Oakland Police
Welfare Committee
200 sq. ft.

Beckett & Federighi
200 sq. ft.

John O'Shea
200 sq. ft.

Chabot P.T.A. Chabot School
200 sq. ft.

Paramount-Built-In
Fixture Company
200 sq. ft.

Claremont Jr. High Students
200 sq. ft.

Production Workers Local
#1566 of Oakland
200 sq. ft.

Joe Donovan
200 sq. ft.

Santa Fe School
200 sq. ft.

El Dorado Oil Works
200 sq. ft.

Virtuoso Club
200 sq. ft.

Embassy Club
200 sq. ft.

Jesse Waller
200 sq. ft.

Claremont Jr. High Faculty
106 sq. ft.

Golden State Employees
101 sq. ft.

Dick, Judy and Jimmie Botto
100 sq. ft.

M. A. Groth
100 sq. ft.

Oscar Nelson
100 sq. ft.

Rockridge P.T.A.
100 sq. ft.

Howard O. Welty
100 sq. ft.

C. Breschi
100 sq. ft.

Bruce Holman
100 sq. ft.

New Liberty Market
100 sq. ft.

Jack Kiernan & John Ronch
100 sq. ft.

Johnny F. Williams
100 sq. ft.

Buon Gusto Pastry Co.
100 sq. ft.

Idora Realty Co.
100 sq. ft.

Oakland Chapter #7
Intl. Footprint Assn.
100 sq. ft.

William R. Rose
100 sq. ft.

Caporgno & Co.
100 sq. ft.

Lloyd Johnson
Dominick Cherrico
100 sq. ft.

Oakland Chapter #965
Women of the Moose
100 sq. ft.

Gus Rouskas
100 sq. ft.

Claremont Jr. High Faculty
100 sq. ft.

Laundry Workers
Union Local 2
100 sq. ft.

Oscar's
100 sq. ft.

Sabatini's Tunnel Inn
100 sq. ft.

Nello Casazza
100 sq. ft.

James M. Leaver
100 sq. ft.

John J. Pagano & Guy Bellini
100 sq. ft.

R. A. Shuey Creamery
100 sq. ft.

Claremont Jr. High P.T.A.
100 sq. ft.

Len & Bud's Cocktail Lounge
100 sq. ft.

Piedmont Ave. P.T.A.
100 sq. ft.

The Piedmont
100 sq. ft.

Vernon (Joe) Connolly
100 sq. ft.

John H. Ludeman
100 sq. ft.

Cotton Pippin, Emil Pradels,
Nobert Kleinke
100 sq. ft.

Troop #12 Boy Scouts
of America
100 sq. ft.

W. Dean Agnew
100 sq. ft.

Charley Garto &
George Gotelli
100 sq. ft.

Rinaldo Mencarelli
Bill Scozzafava
100 sq. ft.

J. A. Ragghianti
100 sq. ft.

Tom Tuohy
100 sq. ft.

Alameda County Building
Trades Council
100 sq. ft.

George's Steak House
100 sq. ft.

August J. Miller
100 sq. ft.

Bud & Doris Richards
100 sq. ft.

Charlie Tye
100 sq. ft.

Alfred Hart Distilleries
100 sq. ft.

Golden Gate Girls Club
100 sq. ft.

Capt. David C. Minney
100 sq. ft.

Red Top Electric Co.
100 sq. ft.

Vernetti's Town House
100 sq. ft.

Capt. Fred R. Barbeau
100 sq. ft.

Good Hope Lodge #29
F. & A. M.
100 sq. ft.

Montclair P.T.A.
100 sq. ft.

Lowell Reed
100 sq. ft.

Villa de la Paix
100 sq. ft.

Lou Bittner
100 sq. ft.

Bert Griffin
100 sq. ft.

R. E. & F. C. Mullen
100 sq. ft.

Rockridge Dads Club
100 sq. ft.

Bud Voigt
100 sq. ft.

Peralta School & P.T.A.
97 sq. ft.

Kehew Family
80 sq. ft.

Santa Fe School
70 sq. ft.

Shattuck Ave. Merchants
70 sq. ft.

F. F. Taylor Co., Inc.
70 sq. ft.

Tanay Club Incorporated
70 sq. ft.

Memorial to Ensign
Jerry Eves U.S.N.R.
60 sq. ft.

Oakland Police, Traffic Div.
60 sq. ft.

Carlos G. White
60 sq. ft.

Order of DeMolay
Rockridge Chapter
52 sq. ft.

Wm. W. Bradly
50 sq. ft.

Emmet J. Guisto
50 sq. ft.

Kiwanis Club of Emeryville
50 sq. ft.

Chas. G. Trometta
50 sq. ft.

Edward Dullwinkel
50 sq. ft.

Frederick O. Gold
50 sq. ft.

Optimist Club of Oakland
50 sq. ft.

A. Vander Naillen, Jr.
50 sq. ft.

Christensen & Lyons
50 sq. ft.

William J. Hughes
50 sq. ft.

Arthur J. Pitka
50 sq. ft.

Amy Vander Naillen
50 sq. ft.

John & Angelo Conte
50 sq. ft.

I.A.W.L.
50 sq. ft.

Roy D. Pulver
50 sq. ft.

Vittoria Columbo Club
50 sq. ft.

Co-operative Cleaners
50 sq. ft.

Madeline M. Jund
50 sq. ft.

Jo Robertson
50 sq. ft.

Mr. & Mrs. J. H. Witt
50 sq. ft.

Delivery Service Co.
50 sq. ft.

Kelly's
50 sq. ft.

Weston S. Robinson
50 sq. ft.

White & Pollard
50 sq. ft.

Ensign Club
50 sq. ft.

F. S. Klinker
50 sq. ft.

Piedmont Ave. School
Dads Club
50 sq. ft.

Temescal Memorial
Post V.F.W. #7379
50 sq. ft.

L. J. Fischl
50 sq. ft.

Edward M. Larmer
50 sq. ft.

Angelo Rossi
50 sq. ft.

West of Market Girls Club, Inc.
50 sq. ft.

Benny Forman
50 sq. ft.

Laundry Drivers Union
Local #209
50 sq. ft.

Herbert H. Sack
50 sq. ft.

Andy Franichevich
50 sq. ft.

Montclair Women's Club
50 sq. ft.

Abe Sugarman
50 sq. ft.

Women's Auxilary, Ligure Club
50 sq. ft.

R. B. Abbott
50 sq. ft.

Tom Franichevich
50 sq. ft.

Oakland Ball Club
50 sq. ft.

Piedmont Garden & Supply
50 sq. ft.

Alfieri Social Club
50 sq. ft.

Wm. Ghiglieri
50 sq. ft.

Oakland Weldonians
50 sq. ft.

Joey & Jimmy Thomas
50 sq. ft.

Bakery Wagon Drivers &
Salesmen's Union #432
50 sq. ft.

The Truman Company
50 sq. ft.

Plymouth Church Members
47 sq. ft.

Students of Oakland
Washington School
45 sq. ft.

* A wall plaque bearing this statement and list of over 785 names hung inside the front entrance of Studio One until April 2005 when it was removed prior to the building's renovation.

Oakland Aquator Club
41 sq. ft.

Lt. H. A. Calame
40 sq. ft.

Harry Rosenberg
40 sq. ft.

T. N. T. Forum
40 sq. ft.

Ray Towers
40 sq. ft.

Mrs. Grace Galmarino
40 sq. ft.

Anthony Viscovich
40 sq. ft.

Vernon Lantz
40 sq. ft.

S. C. MacBeth
40 sq. ft.

Alfred Mastrelli
40 sq. ft.

C. E. Mills
40 sq. ft.

Mr. & Mrs. Harry H. Nomurs
40 sq. ft.

Marsha M. Mitchell
40 sq. ft.

F. Wellington Morse
40 sq. ft.

C. R. Anderson Tile Co.
40 sq. ft.

Plymouth Church
40 sq. ft.

Ted Beckett
40 sq. ft.

Tom W. Reese
40 sq. ft.

Dr. A. C. Soave
40 sq. ft.

Walter Blumert Co.
40 sq. ft.

Norbert Roesling
40 sq. ft.

Louis C. Cerruti
40 sq. ft.

Tira Furniture Co.
40 sq. ft.

Howard O. Welty
32 sq. ft.

Harrison, Sanford &
Irving Kornfeld
30 sq. ft.

Stephen B. Fiske
30 sq. ft.

Technical High Class of
Bernice H. Hendrickson
30 sq. ft.

C. Wadsworth White
30 sq. ft.

Sarah and Samuel Nassau
30 sq. ft.

Temescal Pharmacy
30 sq. ft.

Mrs. John Traynoy
30 sq. ft.

Ruffatto, Lorette,
Melvin & Margaret
30 sq. ft.

In Memory of Benjamin
Joseph Swanson
26 sq. ft.

George Turkmany
25 sq. ft.

G. T. Campau, Jr.
20 sq. ft.

Samuel A. Reeve
20 sq. ft.

Mrs. Bessie Lane
20 sq. ft.

Mrs. Willis Nelson
20 sq. ft.

Phil Reese Store for Men
20 sq. ft.

Santa Fe P.T.A.
20 sq. ft.

Sorensen's Delicatessen
20 sq. ft.

G. E. Wade
20 sq. ft.

Betty Marie Fallrath in
Memory of her Aunt Clara
20 sq. ft.

L. G. Fallrath in Memory
of his Aunt Clara
20 sq. ft.

Colin Campbell
20 sq. ft.

Nito B. Davi
20 sq. ft.

Joe Graves
20 sq. ft.

Mildred Lane
20 sq. ft.

J. D. Nitson
20 sq. ft.

Mrs. N. S. Pimlott
20 sq. ft.

Santa Fe School
20 sq. ft.

Sportsmens Paradise Club
20 sq. ft.

Richard E. Walpole
20 sq. ft.

Augustans Club
20 sq. ft.

Carl's Temescal Barber
20 sq. ft.

M. A. Brooks
20 sq. ft.

Anthony Chabot School
Dad's Club
20 sq. ft.

Lee Layport
20 sq. ft.

Samuel A. Reeves
20 sq. ft.

Eldridge Pratt, Kenneth
Pratt
20 sq. ft.

Arthur Stern
20 sq. ft.

Womens Legislative Club
20 sq. ft.

Probert Gede
20 sq. ft.

Mr. C. J. Avola
20 sq. ft.

Chapel of the Chimes
20 sq. ft.

Demonte Stove Co.
20 sq. ft.

Guarantee Roofing Co.
20 sq. ft.

Mr. & Mrs. I. S. Leonard
20 sq. ft.

Cristopher Lee Crawford
20 sq. ft.

Daniel Read
20 sq. ft.

Sandra Pratt & Gary Pratt
20 sq. ft.

Mrs. C. B. Stewart
20 sq. ft.

Bruce McCollum
20 sq. ft.

T. Wayne Gibson
20 sq. ft.

Dr. Oscar Stowe
20 sq. ft.

Lyle W. Clements
20 sq. ft.

Chas. & Alvin Detata
20 sq. ft.

Alameda County School
Employees Local 257
20 sq. ft.

Liberty French Bakery Co.
20 sq. ft.

Oakland Telegraph
20 sq. ft.

Serve & Save Mkt.
20 sq. ft.

Francine Salamid
20 sq. ft.

In Memory of John Olmo
Who Gave his Life 7-19-44
20 sq. ft.

M. M. Marshall
20 sq. ft.

Mrs. Emily Green to
Mr. & Mrs. L. O. Green
20 sq. ft.

Biggi Grocery
20 sq. ft.

Eugene L. Cleu
20 sq. ft.

George Edwards
20 sq. ft.

E. W. Hansen Co.
20 sq. ft.

Lunchers Club
20 sq. ft.

Norman Ogilvie
20 sq. ft.

George A. Renner
20 sq. ft.

Wm. H. McGrath
20 sq. ft.

Anga Bjornson
20 sq. ft.

George P. Eberhart
20 sq. ft.

Harriet E. Hawes
20 sq. ft.

David G. Madsen
20 sq. ft.

In Memory of
John W. DeLucchi
20 sq. ft.

Dr. Mauro J. Revelli
20 sq. ft.

Hank Smith
20 sq. ft.

Sid Strom
20 sq. ft.

Brignole & Ghiri
20 sq. ft.

J. H. Fisher
20 sq. ft.

Alex Holt
20 sq. ft.

Police Officers Wives
Social Club
20 sq. ft.

DeGrasse Automotive Service
20 sq. ft.

H. Rogers, M.D.
20 sq. ft.

Gertrude Smart
20 sq. ft.

Dave Symon
20 sq. ft.

Walter T. Sprayberry
Walt's Market
20 sq. ft.

Clifton E. Brooks
20 sq. ft.

Howard Cross
20 sq. ft.

George and Walt's
20 sq. ft.

Alice Jameysen
20 sq. ft.

Miss Margit Walden's 6th
Grade Santa Fe School
20 sq. ft.

Edgar L. Ormsby
20 sq. ft.

Joaquine DeMenezes, Jr.
20 sq. ft.

Tom Slater
20 sq. ft.

T. D. & H. Supply Co.
20 sq. ft.

Mr. & Mrs. O. H. Steinbeck
20 sq. ft.

David F. Brown
20 sq. ft.

A. L. Curshen
20 sq. ft.

Gleason and Co.
20 sq. ft.

Mrs. Essai Kuhn
20 sq. ft.

John W. Morgan
20 sq. ft.

Marjorie W. Peirce
20 sq. ft.

St. Augustine's Club
20 sq. ft.

Mayann Salamid
20 sq. ft.

The Hut
20 sq. ft.

G. E. Wade
20 sq. ft.

M. A. Brooks
20 sq. ft.

Cub Scout Pack #16
20 sq. ft.

Fruit Orchard Market
20 sq. ft.

L. J. Kruse Co.
20 sq. ft.

The Mees
20 sq. ft.

Jim & Bob Pearson
20 sq. ft.

Willis Richardson
20 sq. ft.

Ina M. Schmid
20 sq. ft.

The College Bowl
20 sq. ft.

In Memory of Fred B. Veretto
20 sq. ft.

Kathleen Bulger
20 sq. ft. sq. ft.

D. Damonte
20 sq. ft. sq. ft.

Golden Gate Press
20 sq. ft. sq. ft.

The Nat'l Secretaries Assn.
Lake Merritt Chapter
20 sq. ft.

Motor Service Co.
20 sq. ft.

A. S. Pencovic
20 sq. ft.

Al Rubenstein
20 sq. ft.

M. D. Spellman
20 sq. ft.

Mr. and Mrs. G. F. Twist
20 sq. ft.

Western Notion & Novelty Co.
20 sq. ft.

Mary L. Cady
20 sq. ft.

Mario and Helen Damonte
20 sq. ft.

Ladies Drug Auxiliary
of Alameda County
20 sq. ft.

Oakland Municipal Civil
Service Employee's Assn.
20 sq. ft.

Miss June Gellerman's 5th,
6th Grade Santa Fe School
20 sq. ft.

C. A. Pezzola
20 sq. ft.

S and A Motors
20 sq. ft.

Alice Spellman
20 sq. ft.

Karol Valpreda
20 sq. ft.

Dwain H. White
20 sq. ft.

Engine #8 O.F.D.
14 sq. ft.

Flaviano A. Jucutan
14 sq. ft.

Marlene Ann Petry
12 sq. ft.

Cub Pack 51 Oakland
10 sq. ft.

H. W. Townsend
10 sq. ft.

Boy Scouts of America
Troop 9
10 sq. ft.

H. Tulanian
10 sq. ft.

Boy Scout Troop 53
10 sq. ft.

Gerald Veiluva
10 sq. ft.

Boy Scout Troop 74
10 sq. ft.

Richard Veiluva
10 sq. ft.

Washington School Dad's
Club
10 sq. ft.

G. Veitto
10 sq. ft.

Tecumseh Tribe #62
Improved Order of Red Men
10 sq. ft.

Wyman W. Vernon
10 sq. ft.

In Memory of
Armin Henry Cohen
10 sq. ft.

Suzanne, Laurellei Westaway
10 sq. ft.

Maude L. Williams
10 sq. ft.

East Bay Mineral Society Inc.
10 sq. ft.

John Albarello
10 sq. ft.

James P. Wilson
10 sq. ft.

Peter Perata
10 sq. ft.

Mrs. Wirsching
10 sq. ft.

Faith Thurmond
10 sq. ft.

S. F. Worswick
10 sq. ft.

R. F. Throckmorton
10 sq. ft.

Mrs. Myra Wong
10 sq. ft.

Patti Tobin
10 sq. ft.

L. A. Wright
10 sq. ft.

Richard Tocchini
10 sq. ft.

Paul H. Phillips II
10 sq. ft.

Julie Rydos
10 sq. ft.

Carl E. Simmon
10 sq. ft.

Ronald George Souza
10 sq. ft.

Joseph Abood
10 sq. ft.

Ben Benjamin
10 sq. ft.

David M. Brown
10 sq. ft.

Gary G. Claussenius
10 sq. ft.

Dick's Hamburgers
10 sq. ft.

Katherine Gannon
10 sq. ft.

Gerald Hardt
10 sq. ft.

L. E. Johnson
10 sq. ft.

G. M. Letchworth
10 sq. ft.

Joseph J. Veretto
10 sq. ft.

F. P. Robinson
10 sq. ft.

Mrs. Ridgeway Smith
10 sq. ft.

Elaine & Sharon Selle
10 sq. ft.

C. Ronald Smith, M.D.
10 sq. ft.

Wm. J. Voss
10 sq. ft.

Mr. & Mrs. Matzman
10 sq. ft.

Mr. & Mrs. C. Alberti
10 sq. ft.

Walter E. Bannwarth
10 sq. ft.

Joe Bongiovanni
10 sq. ft.

Mr. & Mrs. Syd Cohen
10 sq. ft.

Alfred Delucchi
10 sq. ft.

C. W. Erickson
10 sq. ft.

Frank S. Fresia
10 sq. ft.

W. Joe Graves
10 sq. ft.

O. Y. M. Hallerstede
10 sq. ft.

Harold Holroyd
10 sq. ft.

Ward Kammeree
10 sq. ft.

Mr. Charles Lamberti
10 sq. ft.

Mr. & Mrs. O. M. Mauder
10 sq. ft.

Ernest James Porter, Jr.
10 sq. ft.

Louis A. Sanchez
10 sq. ft.

W. L. Sims
10 sq. ft.

Earl Stark
10 sq. ft.

Joseph Addiego
10 sq. ft.

Helen Benjamin
10 sq. ft.

Johnny Bushell
10 sq. ft.

Homer L. Colvin, Jr.
10 sq. ft.

Capt. L. J. Divine
10 sq. ft.

Louis Garbarino
10 sq. ft.

E. W. Hawkins
10 sq. ft.

Ralph Johnson
10 sq. ft.

Bert Lever
10 sq. ft.

G. L. Small
10 sq. ft.

Russell Pike
10 sq. ft.

Edward M. White
10 sq. ft.

Fred Rau
10 sq. ft.

Alex Ponchione
10 sq. ft.

Herbert Stearns
10 sq. ft.

Neal Young
10 sq. ft.

Louis Alberti
10 sq. ft.

Wm. E. Barkis
10 sq. ft.

D. M. Bonsack
10 sq. ft.

R. Dudley Conness
10 sq. ft.

Mr. & Mrs. Mario DeLucchi
10 sq. ft.

George F. Ewing
10 sq. ft.

Richard & Jon Gai
10 sq. ft.

Art Graziano
10 sq. ft.

Edward F. Hansen
10 sq. ft.

Rev. George H. Holt
10 sq. ft.

Arnold, Elizabeth, Donna,
Johnnie & Arlene Kangas
10 sq. ft.

Larry LeGallee
10 sq. ft.

G. McElhinney
10 sq. ft.

Lucy Pradels
10 sq. ft.

Henry S. Savage, Jr.
10 sq. ft.

Mrs. Ethel Slater
10 sq. ft.

Mark John Stefani
10 sq. ft.

Norman M. Abner
10 sq. ft.

Mrs. Mary Berande
10 sq. ft.

Doug & Cody Burnett
10 sq. ft.

Richard Coffin
10 sq. ft.

Jack Donoviel
10 sq. ft.

Bruce E. Gates
10 sq. ft.

Jack Henning
10 sq. ft.

Tad Jones
10 sq. ft.

Mr. & Mrs. Levinson
10 sq. ft.

Joseph Sledje
10 sq. ft.

Mr. & Mrs. Walter Weir
10 sq. ft.

C. L. Monge
10 sq. ft.

Fred Orsburn
10 sq. ft.

Sunya Shellhammer
10 sq. ft.

Silver Lion
10 sq. ft.

Mr. Frank Stockholm
10 sq. ft.

Louis Alberti
10 sq. ft.

Herbert L. Beach
10 sq. ft.

Anne M. Bradley
10 sq. ft.

Frank Connolly
10 sq. ft.

Mrs. C. F. DeWolf & E. A. Rix
10 sq. ft.

And. Fada
10 sq. ft.

Geraldine Galletti
10 sq. ft.

Marcello Graziano
10 sq. ft.

Mrs. C. Hardt
10 sq. ft.

Christian C. Holtum
10 sq. ft.

Robert J. Kelley
10 sq. ft.

Mary Virginia & Joel Lewis
10 sq. ft.

Harry McIntosh, Jr.
10 sq. ft.

Myron Probert
Edward R. Horton
10 sq. ft.

Mr. & Mrs. William Savage
10 sq. ft.

E. T. Smallwood
10 sq. ft.

Paul L. Stevenson
10 sq. ft.

John Antraccoli, Jr.
10 sq. ft.

Berma's
10 sq. ft.

Philip Burnstein
10 sq. ft.

Lovell A. Colvin
10 sq. ft.

Wm. Dornenburg
10 sq. ft.

Cornielus R. Gift
10 sq. ft.

Harry Hennings
10 sq. ft.

David A. Kashubeck
10 sq. ft.

Mrs. Mary Lewis
10 sq. ft.

Donald Reidt
10 sq. ft.

Mary Sprott
10 sq. ft.

Mrs. Owens
10 sq. ft.

Joan & Marie Ripley
10 sq. ft.

Dominic Romano
10 sq. ft.

Gordon G. Wadsworth
10 sq. ft.

Mrs. Barbara Rahm
10 sq. ft.

Mrs. Charles Allen
10 sq. ft.

Mr. & Mrs. Scott Beamer
10 sq. ft.

Lloyd L. Brown
10 sq. ft.

Angus Couser
10 sq. ft.

Thelma Dick
10 sq. ft.

Margie Fanelli
10 sq. ft.

Thomas L. Galletti
10 sq. ft.

Will W. Green
10 sq. ft.

N. L. Henderson
10 sq. ft.

Jack Hotchkiss
10 sq. ft.

Beatrice Kempf
10 sq. ft.

Edward W. Long
10 sq. ft.

Dr. Harold Meredith
10 sq. ft.

Donald H. Pryds
10 sq. ft.

Russell Schumachar
10 sq. ft.

Herald Smith
10 sq. ft.

Edward Stumpf
10 sq. ft.

Aquator Club
10 sq. ft.

Lt. Herman Bernstein
10 sq. ft.

Walter L. Burrill
10 sq. ft.

Phebe Cramer
10 sq. ft.

T. Douglas
10 sq. ft.

Mr. & Mrs. C. Giovannetti
10 sq. ft.

Syd Henry
10 sq. ft.

M. J. Kerins
10 sq. ft.

Shirley & Jimmey Lewis
10 sq. ft.

Leslie C. Smith &
Mrs. C. Smith
10 sq. ft.

Diane Stearns
10 sq. ft.

Neva Verna Rogers
10 sq. ft.

Thomas N. Welch
10 sq. ft.

James K. Robertson
10 sq. ft.

Chief Robert P. Tracy
10 sq. ft.

Nick D. Wirtz
10 sq. ft.

E. L. Anderson
10 sq. ft.

Ted Beckett
10 sq. ft.

Miss Phyllis Brown
10 sq. ft.

E. E. Cowles
10 sq. ft.

Jos. Dimarci
10 sq. ft.

Gail Ferris
10 sq. ft.

Raymond & Norma Galliani
10 sq. ft.

J. B. Greenwood
10 sq. ft.

Al Hendrickson
10 sq. ft.

Robert Hudson
10 sq. ft.

Mrs. K. R. Kerriggan
10 sq. ft.

Bruno Lorenzi
10 sq. ft.

Mike Guisto Miller
10 sq. ft.

Florence S. Ragle
10 sq. ft.

Ernest A. Scoffone
10 sq. ft.

Mr. & Mrs. Maurice D. Smith
10 sq. ft.

Anne and Chas. Sutherland
10 sq. ft.

Babcock's
10 sq. ft.

John Blaisdell
10 sq. ft.

Earl Caldwell
10 sq. ft.

Dr. J. A. Crane
10 sq. ft.

David M. Duckworth
10 sq. ft.

Joseph Goody
10 sq. ft.

Mrs. Ruby Hildebrand
10 sq. ft.

Mrs. R. L. Kittle
10 sq. ft.

Valerie Lewis
10 sq. ft.

Emil Risi
10 sq. ft.

Ronald Miller
10 sq. ft.

Mr. & Mrs. B. O'Reilly
10 sq. ft.

Alice P. Muller
10 sq. ft.

Timothy Mathews
10 sq. ft.

Doris Ruby
10 sq. ft.

Anna A. Meyer
10 sq. ft.

Robert J. Anderson
10 sq. ft.

Mrs. Don R. Benaliza
10 sq. ft.

Louis Capellini
10 sq. ft.

John Cuneo
10 sq. ft.

Danny Drake
10 sq. ft.

Joan Ferris
10 sq. ft.

Robert S. Geen
10 sq. ft.

Mr. & Mrs. Lawrence E. Grey
10 sq. ft.

Virginia Hart
10 sq. ft.

H. T. Hultgren
10 sq. ft.

Mrs. H. C. Kibbe
10 sq. ft.

Judy Low
10 sq. ft.

Gray Minor
10 sq. ft.

Lee T Ralph
10 sq. ft.

Mr. & Mrs. Terry Scoffone
10 sq. ft.

Wilburn O. Smith
10 sq. ft.

Byrnes Sports Shop
10 sq. ft.

Clare Bain
10 sq. ft.

George Block
10 sq. ft.

Lowell Caldwell
10 sq. ft.

Dr. Gerald L. Crenshaw
10 sq. ft.

Kathleen L. Duckworth
10 sq. ft.

Frank Goria
10 sq. ft.

George E. Hogan
10 sq. ft.

Garrett F. Kyle
10 sq. ft.

Elizabeth Linquest
10 sq. ft.

Marion Scherling
10 sq. ft.

Mrs. Catarina Oldano
10 sq. ft.

Theresa O'Neill
10 sq. ft.

Morlene Miller
10 sq. ft.

Joseph Pratt
10 sq. ft.

"The Swans"
10 sq. ft.

Hal Ruby
10 sq. ft.

Chas. Arregotti
10 sq. ft.

Helen H. Beever
10 sq. ft.

Amelia Caviero
10 sq. ft.

Gary Donal Cunial
10 sq. ft.

Terry Drake
10 sq. ft.

R. D. Ferris
10 sq. ft.

Shirley & Marylin Gergens
10 sq. ft.

Emmet Louis Guisto
10 sq. ft.

Herman H. Harris
10 sq. ft.

Edgar S. Hurley
10 sq. ft.

Mr. & Mrs. G. E. Kiessling
10 sq. ft.

Mr. & Mrs. Remo Lucchetti
10 sq. ft.

Mr. & Mrs. W. W. Mitchell
10 sq. ft.

Raymond Razzano
10 sq. ft.

W. C. Seiffert
10 sq. ft.

Earl J. Smyth, Sr.
10 sq. ft.

Claremont Liquor Store
10 sq. ft.

G. Ballestrasse
10 sq. ft.

Manuel Borges
10 sq. ft.

Leni Campamenosi
10 sq. ft.

Mr. & Mrs. G. B. Crepsey, Jr.
10 sq. ft.

Stan Emery
10 sq. ft.

Ernestine Green
10 sq. ft.

J. F. Hogan
10 sq. ft.

Mrs. Rose Lanzo
10 sq. ft.

Mr. & Mrs. H. J. Loomis
10 sq. ft.

Ottar C. Moe
10 sq. ft.

Mrs. Edith Parle
10 sq. ft.

Mrs. M. Wittmer
10 sq. ft.

Barry Netherwood
10 sq. ft.

Isidore Sherman
10 sq. ft.

Mrs. Crawford White
10 sq. ft.

G. W. "Bud" Roe
10 sq. ft.

Joan Ann Arri
10 sq. ft.

Norman Berge
10 sq. ft.

Domingo Caviero
10 sq. ft.

Phillip Dabel
10 sq. ft.

Dr. Walter Durst
10 sq. ft.

T. J. Filis
10 sq. ft.

Max Gevertz
10 sq. ft.

Martha V. Guisto
10 sq. ft.

Mr. & Mrs. Harrisonryker
10 sq. ft.

L. L. Isenhour
10 sq. ft.

G. W. Kiessling
10 sq. ft.

Mr. & Mrs. Vincent Lucchetti
10 sq. ft.

Veteran World War II
Thos. J. Morris
10 sq. ft.

Jon Reese
10 sq. ft.

Marguerite W. Seiple
10 sq. ft.

Isabel G. Snedigar
10 sq. ft.

Handicrafters Hobby Shop
10 sq. ft.

Mr. Emil Barabino
10 sq. ft.

Elenor Bosshart
10 sq. ft.

Lt. L. M. Carroll
10 sq. ft.

Felix & Francis Croce
10 sq. ft.

B. Ferro
10 sq. ft.

Fernando Guidi
10 sq. ft.

Rose Hotchkiss
10 sq. ft.

H. Laurence Larsen
10 sq. ft.

A. E. Lucas
10 sq. ft.

Albert V. Monge
10 sq. ft.

M. H. Stevens
10 sq. ft.

Angelo Orsolini
10 sq. ft.

Anson P. Wright
10 sq. ft.

Giovanni Moglia
10 sq. ft.

Patricia Jane Rice
10 sq. ft.

Stanley Oldrup
10 sq. ft.

Richard John Arri
10 sq. ft.

Beatrice Beronio
10 sq. ft.

Arthur Chamberlin
10 sq. ft.

Mr. & Mrs. C. B. Dami
10 sq. ft.

Dr. Fred N. Eaton
10 sq. ft.

William J. Finn
10 sq. ft.

Jean E. Gilmore
10 sq. ft.

Henry Gutte, Jr.
10 sq. ft.

Kendall and H.V. Haselhurst
10 sq. ft.

William Jacks
10 sq. ft.

Jack S. Killin
10 sq. ft.

Paul Luyhen
10 sq. ft.

Shirley Morrison
10 sq. ft.

Chris A. Revelli
10 sq. ft.

Edward H. Siems
10 sq. ft.

Mr. & Mrs. Paul Spier
10 sq. ft.

Menefee Bros.
10 sq. ft.

Joseph Batori
10 sq. ft.

Roy Bouander
10 sq. ft.

William E. Chainey
10 sq. ft.

John Cuneo
10 sq. ft.

Philip Fisher
10 sq. ft.

Roy Guidi
10 sq. ft.

Dr. Howard Huenergardt
10 sq. ft.

Chet Larson
10 sq. ft.

Robert A. Manildi
10 sq. ft.

Mildred Snyder
10 sq. ft.

Mr. & Mrs. C. W. Prids
10 sq. ft.

John Vetter
10 sq. ft.

Taylor Mathews
10 sq. ft.

Carrie D. Wagner
10 sq. ft.

Andrew C. Panella
10 sq. ft.

Mr. & Mrs. J. L. Backstrom
10 sq. ft.

Valerie Bertone
10 sq. ft.

Ralph Chamberlin
10 sq. ft.

Mrs. F. J. Daniels
10 sq. ft.

Albert Ebli
10 sq. ft.

William N. Finn
10 sq. ft.

Jacqueline Glasser
10 sq. ft.

Major J. A. Habegger
10 sq. ft.

Herbert Hickman
10 sq. ft.

Don Jamieson
10 sq. ft.

Floyd A. King
10 sq. ft.

Joe & Teresa Marengo
10 sq. ft.

Clyde Mowdy
10 sq. ft.

Bert W. Reynolds
10 sq. ft.

J. P. Silva
10 sq. ft.

Troy, Paul & David Spongberg
10 sq. ft.

Dick Taylor
10 sq. ft.

Mrs. M. Batori
10 sq. ft.

The Boyers
10 sq. ft.

J. Cavanaugh
10 sq. ft.

Shirley Jean Dahel
10 sq. ft.

John Fonzeno
10 sq. ft.

Paul von Hatch
10 sq. ft.

Bernard Jensen
10 sq. ft.

Joseph R. Lawrence
10 sq. ft.

Radio Cash Market
10 sq. ft.

Michael E. Roe
10 sq. ft.

Walter S. Woodward
10 sq. ft.

Mr. Hal W. Wakefield
10 sq. ft.

Carol A. Reidt
10 sq. ft.

Mr. & Mrs. Geo. Powles
10 sq. ft.

Mrs. A. Pedersen
10 sq. ft.

George Balke
10 sq. ft.

James C. Bezpales
10 sq. ft.

C. W. Chan
10 sq. ft.

Mrs. W. Day
10 sq. ft.

Wm. Ebli
10 sq. ft.

Jimmie Fitzwater
10 sq. ft.

George Y. Gong
10 sq. ft.

K. D. Haberern
10 sq. ft.

Maymie Hitchcock
10 sq. ft.

Anne Johnson
10 sq. ft.

Mr. & Mrs. Krioki
10 sq. ft.

Mrs. M. L. Marr
10 sq. ft.

Dr. & Mrs. A. P. Muller
10 sq. ft.

Tony Roderick
10 sq. ft.

Emil Serena
10 sq. ft.

Cyril K. Sprinkling
10 sq. ft.

Mr. Yuen Tang
10 sq. ft.

Sue Ann & Stephen Bayley
10 sq. ft.

Elliott Michael Breuer
10 sq. ft.

Bill Chandler
10 sq. ft.

Damele Family
10 sq. ft.

Donald Ford
10 sq. ft.

A. E. Hall
10 sq. ft.

E. A. Jensen, D.D.S.
10 sq. ft.

Mr. Henry Leiosen
10 sq. ft.

Mr. N. F. Marshall
10 sq. ft.

Taft Ave. Boys Club
10 sq. ft.

Parkers
10 sq. ft.

J. M. Rush
10 sq. ft.

Jim Sergeant
10 sq. ft.

Harry Otto
10 sq. ft.

Grace Walker
10 sq. ft.

Steve Persoglio
10 sq. ft.

Ernest James Ball
10 sq. ft.

Mr. & Mrs. A. C. Blackmun
10 sq. ft.

Mr. and Mrs. A. L.
Christiansen & Nancy
10 sq. ft.

Gene DeAlessi
10 sq. ft.

Frank & Cora Enright
10 sq. ft.

Mrs. Jules C. Fisher
10 sq. ft.

Theodore H. Gordon
H. Koplan
10 sq. ft.

Betty B. Hadden
10 sq. ft.

Bert Hoffschneider
10 sq. ft.

Gilbert R. Jones
10 sq. ft.

George LaHoe
10 sq. ft.

R. C. H. Martin
10 sq. ft.

Mrs. E. J. Murray
10 sq. ft.

Romiti Elasa
10 sq. ft.

Parnell Shuttleworth
10 sq. ft.

P. Votto & Dr. Soave
10 sq. ft.

Jos. D. Thomas
10 sq. ft.

Behren's Appliances
10 sq. ft.

Mr. Brignole
10 sq. ft.

L. P. Clark
10 sq. ft.

John & Virginia Delucchi
10 sq. ft.

Jos. J. Foster
10 sq. ft.

Mr. & Mrs. M. L. Hamlin
10 sq. ft.

Miss Henrietta A. Johnson
10 sq. ft.

Dick Ming Leong
10 sq. ft.

Henry J. Mason
10 sq. ft.

Radio Center
10 sq. ft.

Quan Store
10 sq. ft.

Dick and Archie Newsom
10 sq. ft.

Chas. Oberto
10 sq. ft.

Dr. W. R. Odell
10 sq. ft.

June Ogilvie
10 sq. ft.

Capt. & Mrs
Charles Peterson
10 sq. ft.

Capt. Julius Blatt
10 sq. ft.

Joseph H. Bond & Family
10 sq. ft.

Wm. Douglas Clarke
10 sq. ft.

C. A. DeGrace
10 sq. ft.

E. A. Epperson
10 sq. ft.

C. F. Frane
10 sq. ft.

Alleen V. Graves II
10 sq. ft.

Daniel Kyle Haley
10 sq. ft.

Vernie Hoffschneider
10 sq. ft.

David Joyce
10 sq. ft.

Frank Lallement
10 sq. ft.

Miss Jeanne Mauder
10 sq. ft.

Marshall F. Peterson
10 sq. ft.

We understood that the North Oakland Recreation Center would be primarily for the benefit of those living in North Oakland; but it was like a branch library—you have the locals who use it, but it's available to the entire city. Beyond this, we didn't get into the center's specific use. We left that to the Recreation Department to decide.

It Made You Feel Good

Temescal Pool, 1949. *Courtesy of the Oakland History Room*

There were quite a number of people at the ceremony for the opening of the Temescal Pool, which was in the spring of 1949. At the time, the pool had been completed, but the recreation center had not yet been readied and the building was still unoccupied. I remember speaking at the dedication of the swimming pool. "This is great," I said. "You built a beautiful pool, but you haven't complied with the terms of the gift. Unless you finish the recreation center building—and use it for recreational purposes—the land, building, and pool will come back to us." I said it in humor, but also to jack them up, because the city still had a ways to go before finishing.

In the 1950s, I became a lot busier with my practice and had more limited time than before. I also got married in 1950, and then we had a daughter, so I had a lot more responsibilities.

At the time, the North Oakland Recreation Center received as much recognition as any area-wide project. There was a plaque that was put up in the building, listing the board of directors of the Recreation Center Committee of the North Oakland Area Council. We had a community that really came together, and that was quite an accomplishment. It made you feel good to do it. ✦

Mayor Clifford E. Rishell and Councilman Douglas Sweeney will participate in an "open house" marking the opening of the North Oakland Recreation Center at 365 45th Street from 2 to 4 p.m. Sunday. . . .

Beginning at 2 p.m., the program will feature the presentation of a plaque to the center bearing the names of all those who contributed $5 or more to the purchase of the property.

Entertainment will include a concert by the Technical High School band, a folk dancing demonstration by the Bushrod juniors and seniors, and a swimming exhibition by the Aquators in Temescal Pool.

Oakland Tribune
September 17, 1949

Joan Corbelli (left) and Shirley Haesloop try out the new Temescal Pool at its dedication, April 12, 1949. *Courtesy of the Oakland History Room*

There was that certain day [in 1919] . . . that the City Council discovered recreation officials were violating the charter by operating a community program for all age groups, from tots to grandmothers, when they should have been conducting activities for youngsters only, as decreed by the "Children's" Playground Commission. . . . [Jay B.] Nash was ordered to keep all grownups out of play areas from that day forth and when he protested the council threatened to stop "all public money for recreation." Never daunted, the crusading leader went to his staunch ally, Chief of Police John Lynch, with details of the controversy and then quietly asked for 250 officers to guard every gate to every play area (there were now more than 30) in the city—to keep out all adults. . . . The Chief stared for a moment, raised a quizzical brow and as quietly answered, "My friend, you'd better get the charter amended." . . . which is exactly what the superintendent did.

Oakland Tribune
May 4, 1952

Girls volleyball in the early days of Oakland playgrounds. *Courtesy of the Oakland History Room*

Carol Pulcifer

Zelma Carol Pulcifer's long association with the Oakland Parks and Recreation Department began in about 1925, when at the age of 14, she moved with her mother and sister to Oakland. "My affiliation with the Department goes way back to Oakland camps, when I was a teenager, and then when I was a counselor. I also worked all during college as a playground supervisor."

After graduating from UC Berkeley, Carol (as most people know her) taught high school English for seven years and then, with the outbreak of World War II, spent three years in Europe with the Red Cross. After the war, she returned to the Bay Area, where she worked briefly for Hayward's Park and Recreation district before being hired as a general supervisor in the Oakland Recreation Department. That was in 1947, and for her, "coming back to Oakland was like old home week."

The community service philosophy, inspired by the settlement house movement in Chicago and other eastern cities in the early 1900s and brought to Oakland by some of the city's early recreation leaders, continued to distinguish the Oakland Recreation Department and how it viewed its mission. The Studio One arts program, established the same year Carol came to the department, was just one of the many innovations that resulted from this philosophy.

Over the next 25 years—until she retired in 1972—Carol witnessed and helped bring about many other innovative programs in the Oakland Recreation Department. To an unprecedented extent, her department expanded its neighborhood programs, constructed new recreation centers and pools throughout the city, and built a team of highly skilled and dedicated staff. (In 1970, her department merged with the Parks Department to form the Department of Parks and Recreation.) During this period, recreation as a profession also matured. Whereas there had been no recreation major available at UC Berkeley in 1930 when Carol was a student, twenty years later undergraduate majors and graduate programs in recreation were being established at universities throughout the country.

Since retiring, Carol has remained active in numerous volunteer cultural and service organizations. She makes her home in Oakland.

The Spirit of the City

When World War II ended, there was an upwelling of interest in Oakland in the potential of recreation. The city's recreation programs had been restrained by the war for so long. Not only had materials been unavailable, but so many young men had been gone, which meant that recreation center directors were scarce. The verve to make up for lost time was part of the spirit of the entire city. People really wanted to build swimming pools and recreation centers. Not long before I got there, a bond measure had been passed that funded the building of five municipal swimming pools. So, we now had both the spirit and the means to do it.

Nineteen forty-five marked momentous milestones for organized recreation when voters sanctioned the bond issue and end of the war followed in August. A total of $1,023,000 of the bond fund was allocated to recreation and plans for an immediate expansion program were under way the following year.

Oakland Tribune, May 4, 1952

The philosophy in the Oakland Recreation Department at the time was also unique. In the beginning of the 1900s, the settlement house movement in the east had developed a lot of group work practices for serving neighborhoods, and mothers and children, particularly in settings where there were immigrants. Fortunately, early organizers in our department—such as Ethel Moore and Jay B. Nash—brought these ideas to Oakland, and this philosophy set the tone for the entire Recreation Department over the next several decades. In 1945, Bob Crawford was hired as Superintendent of Recreation, and the same year Alta Bunker became Supervisor of Programs. Together they furthered this approach, creating a team of highly trained recreation professionals whose mission went well beyond the sports-oriented programs of other cities.

Jay B. Nash
Courtesy of the Oakland History Room

The thinking behind it, for example, was not, "We need to have a baseball team," or "We need to have a swimming pool," but, "We need to be in the neighborhoods, serving people." We had sports, of course, but even there, our thinking was to protect kids from the evils of having too much emphasis placed on molding them to be the best pitcher on the team. Many parents were motivated by wanting their kid to be a champion, when maybe that wasn't what their kid needed. Our philosophy was not: pare down until you've only got the champions; rather, it was: the more kids you could serve, the better. So, instead of Little League, Alta Bunker suggested a different organization for Oakland, one that used a system of evaluating kids' abilities and then setting up comparable teams to play each other. This meant that everyone could participate. The recreation centers, the athletics and aquatics departments, the day camps—they were all committed to developing their programs according to this philosophy.

Alta Bunker
Courtesy of the Oakland History Room

It was also a unique situation in Oakland then because the needs of many of Oakland's communities were dramatically changing. In Brookfield Village in East Oakland, enrollment at the school one June was about ninety percent white, and ten percent black. By the next registration, in August, it was just the reverse—ninety percent black.

Background: Studio One logo

The first thing that Alta Bunker and Bob Crawford did was to recruit black people from all over the United States who had the right training in social group work (and in athletics, too) and who were recognized leaders. That was one of the solutions to the changing needs—to get black leadership into the community. There again, our thinking wasn't simply to keep kids off the street or get them playing baseball. It had to with serving people in the ways they needed.

Robert Crawford
Courtesy of the Oakland History Room

It took a lot to persuade taxpayers and the city council that all of this was worthwhile. People didn't think that way. They thought recreation was a good thing, because it kept kids off the street. There was little understanding about the deeper role of recreation in people's lives. This included the belief—and the city of Richmond was a model for this in the arts—that adults needed recreation as much as kids needed it. We felt that everybody needed to be able to explore art and music and theater. We also believed that there needed to be a supportive, non-competitive environment in which people could develop these interests. Creating this kind of setting that was dedicated to the arts is what made Studio One unique.

The Kind of Spirit You Loved

As I recall, the original Studio had been started in 1948 at Bushrod Park in North Oakland. There was an old out-shack with one or two kilns, and that's where they did the pottery. Before long they had outgrown their space. By the time I came to the Recreation Department, the North Oakland Recreation Center project was already in the works. It was another one of these after-the-war things. The community was thrilled about the idea, and they were able to do it!

When I was in high school at University High on Grove Street, everybody knew that the building on 45th Street was an orphanage. During the war the Army took it over. It was after the war that the property became available.

Belva Heer (left) and her sister, Mollie Fisher, 2001. They and a third sister, Lois Johnson, lived at the children's home in the 1930s.

My memory is that it was

At the North Oakland Area Council's meeting of last week the go-ahead signal was given to a committee of 30 to purchase the property between 42nd and 45th streets for a recreation center. The enthusiasm of the 75 members present was shown by their unanimous endorsement of the plans. . . .

The center will be dedicated to the veterans of World War II and will be the first such project undertaken by any group in Oakland.

Montclarion, June 5, 1947

When the new Bushrod Recreation Center was completed later in 1948, the Studio Arts and Crafts program was transferred to the east wing of this facility, but being a city-wide rather than a neighborhood service, it remained under the direct supervision of Alta Bunker; whereas the recreation center program . . . remained a part of the District II operation under the supervision of Aleen Graves. Both programs developed amicably. . . .

This tradition of cooperation between the Studio and Center directors, despite the split supervision, continued in 1949 upon completion of the renovation of the 45th Street site, then called the North Oakland Recreation Center. Jean Tracy was given jurisdiction of two rooms, plus office and storage space on the second floor. Abby Schmidt Dodge and her husband, Charles, became resident directors living in an apartment that was later converted to the children's art room and drama office. Both programs flourished in friendship. . . .

Under Ruth Beadle's auspices (1951-1969), many art school students and recent art school graduates became instructors at Studio One. Many of these artists went on to distinguish themselves in their respective media, and they attracted enthusiastic followings. Just a few of the artists that contributed to the high quality of instruction [at Studio One] in the 1950s and 1960s include Robert Arneson, Ralph and Martha Borge, Robert Brady, Viola Frey, Richard Graf, Michael Lopez, Dixon Poirson, Esteban, Eunice and Mark Prieto, Steven de Staebler, Paul Volkening, Peggy Voulkos, and Alice Hauser Wolff.

Studio One Art Center: A Brief History, 1989

Background: Window, Studio One.

the North Oakland community that started the ball rolling, not the Recreation Department. Aleen Graves was the supervisor of recreation centers for what was then District 2. She was very involved in the effort. There were community meetings, and several top leaders in the community were involved.

When the city finally got the North Oakland Recreation Center fixed up in 1949, Alta Bunker insisted that it shouldn't be merely a collection of already existing clubs that used the Center. We also started right off with the plan that the Studio would move into part of the second floor, which would give it plenty more space than it had at Bushrod.

The first coordinator of the Studio was Jean Tracy. It was Jean's influence that attracted very artistic people to the Studio. They really had a strong feeling about themselves, and about art. She had a Bauhaus way of thinking, which emphasized the integrity of the artist's concept—you leave artists alone in their exploration, you don't go and correct them. She was sometimes not too practical, and some of the staff were critical of her Bauhaus approach. But she brought an appreciation of the art-making process, where all of it—the conceiving, doing, and completing of projects—was important. It was Jean's idea to call it Studio One, to call attention to the art.

In 1951, Ruth Beadle came in as director. Ruth was a very practical person. You can imagine that it isn't always easy to work with artists, especially when they have to comply with certain

Ruth Beadle. *Courtesy of the Oakland History Room*

The building at 365-45th Street could be converted with relative economy because it already had elements importantly suitable for the new usage. There were numerous, mostly tall windows. Ceiling heights were substantial. There was quite a variety of different rooms, including a number of sizable ones like the former dormitories and playrooms. There was a parlor with a fireplace, and a dining room with adjacent kitchen. Taken together, such characteristics made the building quite adaptable for heterogeneous recreational use—including art classes needing appropriate studio spaces.

John English, excerpted from the draft application to list Studio One in the National Register of Historic Places, 2005.

Adult ceramics, Studio One, 1954. *Courtesy of the Oakland History Room*

regulations. Ruth was able to ride that horse and still have the Studio set standards that people could understand and follow, whether they were artists or not. For instance, we had a time there when some people were using our kilns to make their own pottery and then sell it elsewhere. When we had to put a stop to that, there were those who threw up their hands, saying, "You're spoiling it!" But Ruth did a good job of facing that kind of problem and achieving a balance that was necessary to have the system work.

Bert Trubody
Courtesy of the Oakland History Room

Bert Trubody was a very creative man in charge of all the Recreation Department maintenance and construction. Bert and all of those men in the shop were really *interested* in the Studio because people were working with *things*. Any time Ruth wanted to get something new, Bert and his crew would manage to get it for the Studio.

At one point, Ruth figured they had the funds—she was always good with the money—for another potter's wheel. Bert came down, looked things over, researched it, and came back saying, "We could *make* one." And instead of one wheel, she got four. But it didn't stop there. There was a studio worker—Ellen was her name—who because of a disability wasn't able to use her foot to work the wheel. So, after Bert delivered those four wheels, he came in one day with a fifth wheel—electric—for Ellen! Of course, when I heard about this I wondered how it was fitting in the budget. So I said to Bert, "Whose budget is this coming out of?" He got reared up a little and said, "I made that wheel on weekends at home, and it didn't cost the department a thing!" That was the kind of spirit you loved, and it didn't matter which job you were in, which layer in the hierarchy; that's what it was like.

Children's ceramics, 1954. *Courtesy of the Oakland History Room*

Junior Theater, 1960. *Courtesy of the Oakland History Room*

In the 1950s, the city established Studio Two at Arroyo Viejo Recreation Center in East Oakland. Unfortunately, Studio Two, which was just as active as Studio One, eventually closed as a result of the city's budget reduction due to Proposition 13. Studio One survived, in part because it had such good volunteers and a solid organization of people behind it. We always had committed, loyal patrons of the Studio, people who were really interested in what happened there, and in supporting it.

Over time, Studio One grew. The apartment upstairs where the recreation center director originally lived became the children's workshop room. The city's drama program came to the building, and eventually Studio One took up both floors. In the mid-1960s the building was renamed the North Oakland Cultural Center.

The Principles Involved

Back then, the whole concept of recreation was changing. But it was a selling job all the way. Every time the city found itself facing a hard financial picture, recreation would be forgotten. Fortunately, we had some people in our department who knew how to fight. They understood the principles involved and could articulate them, and they knew where to take a stand. Alta Bunker was particularly good at that. She was a strong person. I don't know whether we would have had Studio One if it hadn't been for her conviction that this was what the community needed, and that the city had a role in providing it. ✦

Velma Maggiora, O. M. Anwyl and Aldo Guidotti at rededication of Studio One, June 10, 1964.
Courtesy of the Oakland History Room

Background: Pam Ramos, painting class, Studio One, 2005.

The Ladies' Relief Society's Home for Aged Women can be seen in the background as troops and trainees board an Oakland, Antioch & Eastern train at the 40th and Shafter station, 1916. *Photo: J.K. Southerland; Thomas R. Bold Collection*

Sacramento Northern Railway

Changing Times Along Shafter Avenue

Shafter at 41st Street (looking west), circa 1912. *Courtesy of Paul Smith*

Introduction

Back in 1947 when Aldo Guidotti was in the midst of the community fundraising drive to purchase the former children's home, streetcars, as he noted, were still running on Telegraph Avenue. The Key System's extensive network of streetcars and trains included other lines in North Oakland, such as on Claremont, College, Shattuck, Grove, Broadway, 55th Street and 40th Street. Evidence of this remains today in the broader width of many of these commercial avenues, and in several AC Transit bus lines that follow the same routes. But who would guess that passenger and freight trains once rumbled up and down Shafter Avenue through the middle of the Temescal and Rockridge neighborhoods?

Beginning in 1913, from its depot and rail yard at Shafter and 40th Street, the Sacramento Northern—as it came to be called in 1929 after a series of mergers—ran up Shafter, around Lake Temescal, into Montclair, through a tunnel at the top of Shepherd Canyon, and on north to Sacramento and Chico along a route that is considered by some to have been the longest electric interurban line in the country. Today, thanks to historians and generations of "rail fans," we have considerable documentation of the Sacramento Northern in the form of photographs, maps, publications, and videos. However, few physical traces remain of the Sacramento Northern's operations in North Oakland, and so we tend to be unaware of its once large presence in our community.

Car 52, 40th Street and Opal, 1912. *Photo: Cook & Cook; Vernon J. Sappers Collection*

Paul Smith and Don Olsen, as the following interviews with them reveal, were close observers of the Sacramento Northern, and each describes the popularity of interurbans before the ascendancy of the automobile. As Don points out, the growth of the industry was often fueled by real estate interests exploiting the potential of new streetcar and railway lines to open up outlying areas to development. This was the case with Francis Marion "Borax" Smith's Realty Syndicate, whose extensive landholdings in the early decades of the twentieth century included many parcels in and around the still sparsely settled Temescal and Rockridge neighborhoods. (F. M. Smith and partners also owned the Key System, whose official name was the Railway Equipment and Realty Company.) The coming of the Oakland, Antioch and Eastern Railway—predecessor to the Sacramento Northern—and the siting of its station at Shafter and 40th on Realty Syndicate property promised, through this symbiotic relationship, to be a boon to both railway and real estate company.

While countless commuters benefited from the Sacramento Northern, for many people living along Shafter Avenue in 1913 and in later years, the railroad was a mixed blessing. Among other inconveniences were its "carloads of sheep . . . [arousing] residents from their sleep with a chorus of bahs and a high flown stench."* By the 1940s, with Temescal and Rockridge now substantially built up and the automobile in ever-wider use, the various daily annoyances of Sacramento Northern trains and the related fear of depreciating property values grew larger in the minds of those residing on Shafter. In 1947, the Rockridge Improvement Club, which had begun to press the Oakland City Council to shut down the Sacramento Northern operation in North Oakland, purportedly presented a petition signed by thousands of neighbors demanding the removal of the trains. The battle waged until 1957 when the owners of the Sacramento Northern, who themselves had been petitioning for over a decade to relocate the line to West Oakland, finally were granted their request. Before the year was out, the Sacramento Northern station and yard were demolished, the rails along Shafter were torn up and sold for scrap, and the length of Shafter was re-paved.

Shafter Avenue (looking north toward Forest), circa 1950. *Frank Suzio Collection*

It didn't take long for developers to see opportunity in the vacant lots where the station and rail yard had been. Soon, an office building went up on Shafter and 40th where the depot had stood. In 2002, this building was gutted by fire and its charred remains torn down. Again, a developer seized the opportunity, and in the fall of 2005, earth moving equipment rolled onto the site to level the lot for the 30-unit "Temescal Station" condo and townhouse complex. One wonders what remnants of the Sacramento Northern—sections of rail, rusted spikes, unidentifiable fragments of machinery—were unearthed in the process, briefly bringing to light physical traces of a time when trains and streetcars were dependable, affordable, and, as Paul Smith describes, "*the* way to go."

* *The Claremont Press*, August 19, 1960

Rails were laid in 1912 amid a heated franchise battle wherein residents on Shafter Ave. sought to prevent the construction of a railroad before their very doors.... A temporary court order was obtained by the railroad and its rails were quickly laid with the assistance of Key System line crews. As soon as the trolley wire was completed it was energized at 600 volts and Oakland Traction Company's single truck streetcar 52 was leased and run up and down the street to hold the franchise. The single track was laid off center as it was hoped to someday double track the line; this never came to pass.

Interurbans Special 26, 1971

Paul Smith

In 1937, at the age of 14, Paul Smith moved with his family from Piedmont to Oakland's Montclair district. The house they moved into overlooked the Sacramento Northern tracks, and it was then that Paul's fascination with the interurban railway began. Unlike many train enthusiasts whose interests extend to many different railroads, Paul as a teenager and young man was captivated almost exclusively by the Sacramento Northern. The hundreds of photos of the Sacramento Northern which he took and collected between 1938 and the early 1950s are proof of this singular passion. With the responsibilities of a family and career in the 1950s—and as interurban railroads across the country were shutting down—his documentation of the Sacramento Northern tapered off. Yet even today, looking at a two-inch-square, black and white photograph of a Sacramento Northern train taken in 1940, Paul with only a moment's hesitation can tell you the car numbers, direction the train was heading, and where and what time of day the photo was taken.

With a degree in civil engineering from Santa Clara University, Paul has worked as a fire and life safety engineer on projects all over the world. He and his wife, Helen, raised their seven children in Oakland. Since 1974, they have made their home in Greenbrae, Marin County.

Something Was Going On Down There

In about 1937, my family moved to Oakland. Our house was right on the Sacramento Northern line in Montclair, not far from Thornhill Station, near Thornhill and Moraga roads. My room was a sleeping porch that looked right down on the railroad. One night, something was going on down there—there was pounding and yelling and so forth, and it woke me up. I learned that it had been a work train, and that they were repairing the roadbed—which they did at night, when no trains were running. That was what first got my attention, and from then on I was very interested in the Sacramento Northern and its operations.

Sacramento Northern freight, viewed from Paul Smith's sleeping porch, Montclair, circa 1940. *Photo: Paul Smith*

I was around fourteen when I first visited the station on 40th Street and Shafter. It wasn't long after that I took my first ride on the Sacramento Northern. A friend who had already become a rail fan talked me into taking one of those one-dollar roundtrip excursions to Sacramento.

About that time my uncle gave me a Graflex camera to use. I started taking pic-

Sacramento Northern crew, (l-r) Wicks, brakeman; Ernest "Knobby" Knoblock, conductor; Oscar Schindler, motorman, 40th and Shafter, 1941. *Photo: Paul Smith*

tures—I took hundreds. I photographed all parts of the line, between San Francisco and Chico, all of the equipment, rolling stock. I rode the rails a great deal.

I spent a lot of time hanging out at 40th and Shafter, so I knew almost all of the train crews by their first names. I took pictures of all of them and would make extra prints for them. They appreciated it. They were a really nice bunch of people.

All the Way to Chico

An interurban railroad like the Sacramento Northern was one that ran between separate urban communities, as opposed to a streetcar system, which generally ran within a single metropolitan area. The Sacramento Northern ran from the Bay Area to Sacramento and on to Chico. There was an interurban line that ran between Petaluma and Santa Rosa, another which ran from San Jose to Los Gatos—all electrically powered. There were lots of interurbans throughout the U.S. At one time, that was *the* way to go. The Los Angeles area had a huge system. Chicago had several large systems. They were big, medium, small—and almost all of them thriving.

What was eventually consolidated into the Sacramento Northern in 1927 began in 1911 as the Oakland, Antioch and Eastern Railway. Building of the line started in the Port Chicago Area—what was then known as Baypoint—and the railroad pretty much grew from there to Oakland, and from Sacramento, south. They built the line to regular, transcontinental railroad standards, and they ran it according to standard railroad rules. In the beginning, they planned to skirt the Oakland Hills, because all the other railroads had done so. There also had been a great deal of opposition from the public and the City of Oakland to putting a tunnel

Map showing the route of the Sacramento Northern Railway. *Courtesy of Interurbans Special 26*

through the Oakland Hills. But that's the way it went. It was a tough job building that tunnel, and some lives were lost. The tunnel is still there—boarded up but still there. Service from Oakland to Sacramento began in 1913. Within a couple years, you could go all the way to Chico, using the Northern Electric Railway tracks.

In 1920, the Oakland, Antioch and Eastern became the San Francisco Sacramento, and after some more mergers, including with the Northern Electric, the Sacramento Northern Railway was formed in 1929, making one company that ran the entire 180 miles between Oakland and Chico, with branches to Oroville, Marysville, Woodland, Danville, and elsewhere. Actually, at that point they were owned by the Western Pacific Railroad, but they continued to operate as the Sacramento Northern.

40th Street and Telegraph (looking easterly), 1938. *Photo: Ted Wurm*

Shafter and 43th Street (looking south), circa 1940. *Photo: Paul Smith*

Rockridge, above Chabot Road (looking easterly), 1942. *Photo: Paul Smith*

It Went Up Shafter Avenue

The Sacramento Northern ran from the Key Route pier in Oakland. Using Key System tracks, it crossed San Pablo Avenue, ran up Yerba Buena Avenue until it merged with 40th Street, and then followed 40th Street to Shafter, where the Sacramento Northern's main station and a small freight yard were located. From there, it went up Shafter Avenue to College, where there was a stop. It crossed the Key System No. 6 streetcar line on College and continued up Shafter into Rockridge, where there was a siding. Next was Temescal Station, on the north side of Lake Temescal. There was no building, just a sign and a platform where passengers could wait. There was also a siding there, used occasionally by the freight trains. From there it went through the Broadway Terrace area, then across into Thornhill Station, which was on Moraga Road. There were signals where it crossed the old Highway 13—it really disturbed the highway district to have a train cross the highway. The route continued to Montclair Station, which, like Temescal, was just a wide spot with a paved area for passengers. From there it went to the Havens station, which was at the west portal of the tunnel. At Havens there was a fairly well

Lake Temescal stop (at north end of lake), 1937. *Photo: Paul Smith*

Montclair stop, circa 1940. *Photo: Paul Smith*

Havens Station, Montclair hills, 1940. *Courtesy of Bay Area Rails website*

St. Mary's, Moraga, 1940. *Photo: Ted Wurm*

built station, and sidings. There were a few scattered homes in the hills around there at the time, so it had been developed, but not heavily. On the other side of the tunnel was Eastport. From there the line continued down into Redwood Canyon, then to Pinehurst, Moraga Station, St. Mary's College, Lafayette, and on to the north.

The Station at 40th and Shafter

It was a nice, easy grade from the west portal of the tunnel down through Montclair and Rockridge, and from there, Shafter Avenue was a direct route to 40th Street, where they built the station and rail yard. It hadn't been easy to get the franchise from the city to run trains on Shafter, but they got it.

Laying track, upper Shafter Avenue, 1913. *Photo: Cook and Cook; Collection of Vernon J. Sappers*

They'd originally planned to build the shops and switching yard up in Rockridge, at the intersection of Shafter and Chabot, but there was so much opposition from the neighborhood that they never did it. They owned the land there, put a couple of tracks in, and once in a while they'd store a car there, but they hardly ever used it. It was that way until the railroad was abandoned in 1957.

The main reason for terminating at Shafter and 40th Street was because the trains could connect with the Key System and run on Key Systems tracks to the Key pier. From there, Sacramento Northern passengers could take ferries to San Francisco.

It was an odd-looking station at 40th and Shafter. The small depot, which was located on the west side of Shafter, right at 40th Street, was triangular in shape. It was a two-story, wood-frame building. On the ground floor was a ticket office, which had an inside and outside window that made it easy for people to buy their tickets. There was also a baggage check, and a small waiting area that I don't think held more than a dozen people. The interior was natural wood that might have been stained or varnished. The floor was wood, the ceiling was plastered, and the seating was wooden benches. Upstairs were offices and the switching tower where they controlled the switches to the tracks in and out of the yard. There was nothing luxurious about the station, though there was a little food stand just across

Sacramento Northern station, 40th and Shafter (looking north), 1940. *Photo: Ted Wurm*

Boyscouts waiting for train, Sacramento Northern depot, 40th and Shafter (looking south), 1938. *Photo: Paul Smith*

Shafter that served refreshments. There was a nice lady who worked there. She sold not just soft drinks and sandwiches, but magazines, newspapers—everything. I believe it closed after passenger service was discontinued in 1941.

The trains came in on the west side of the station and loaded the passengers out in the open on the train's east side. There were two tracks there, one for eastbound and one for westbound trains. There was a much bigger building immediately to the west of the tracks that housed the main shops and other offices.

Sacramento Northern shops, 40th and Shafter (looking west), 1940. *Photo: Ted Wurm*

The rail yard itself was quite small, but they made do. There was a siding for the freight shed, which was on the east side of Shafter along 40th Street. The little refreshment stand was at the west end of that building. On the corner of 41st and Opal was another building that housed the paint shop. They also stored a car or two in there and almost always a small wrecker and the portable electric generator on rails, to be moved if necessary in case of, say, a derailment. The rest of the yard was used to make up passenger trains, and, at night, freight trains.

Back when I hung around there, the surrounding Temescal neighborhood was working class, white, quiet. Shafter Avenue was narrow. There were no stoplights on Shafter then—only stop signs at 42nd Street and 45th Street. There was just one track, which was off-centered, on the west side. If somebody didn't park close enough to the curb,

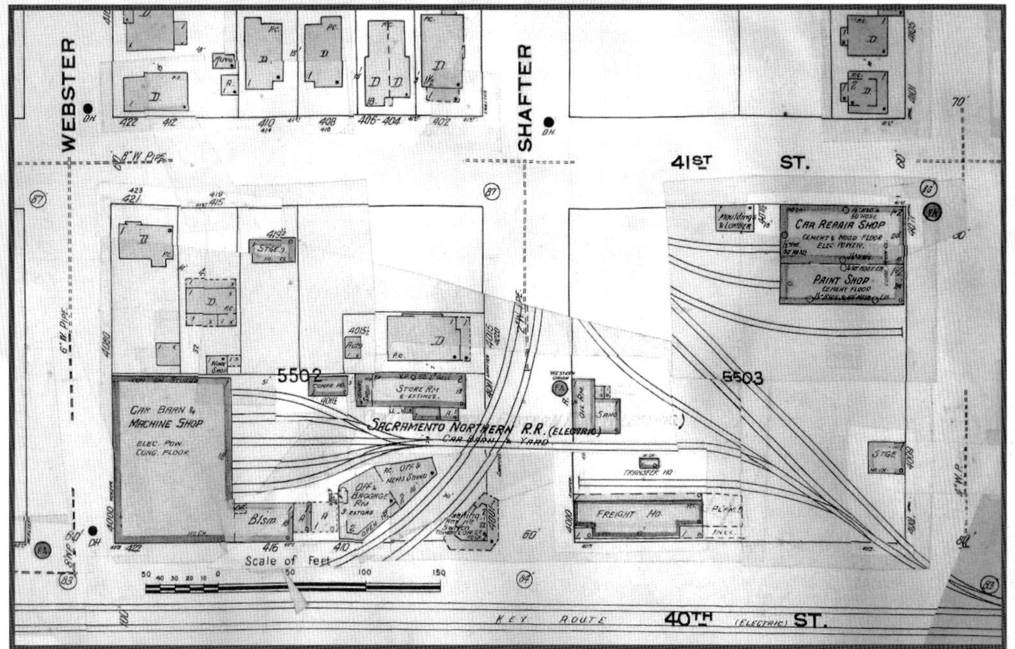

Map (detail) showing Sacramento Northern Railway station and yard, Sanborn Insurance Map Co., 1911–1932. *Courtesy of Oakland History Room*

40th Street, between Webster and Shafter (looking westerly). *Photo: Paul Smith*

circa 1940

Shafter Avenue at 41st Street (looking north). *Photo: Paul Smith*

40th Street, between Webster and Shafter (looking westerly).

Shafter Avenue at 41st Street (looking north).

Oakland, Antioch & Eastern depot, 40th and Shafter (looking west), 1913. *Courtesy of the Oakland History Room*

Troops and trainees board an OA&E train, 40th and Shafter, 1916. *Photo: J.K. Southerland; Thomas R. Bold Collection*

Boyscout group boarding train, Sacramento Northern depot, 40th and Shafter, 1938. *Photo: Paul Smith*

a train couldn't get by without a collision. The train crews kept a very, very close eye out to make sure they'd clear any parked vehicle. If they couldn't clear, they had a terrible problem. It didn't happen often, but often enough to irritate the crew. Otherwise, I don't remember hearing about any vicious complaints, though once in a while there would be one about the freight trains going by at night.

I read articles, from before my time, about freight cars that got away. One time a gravel car collided with a streetcar at College and Shafter. Another time, a freight car got away, ran off the track at College, and crashed into a real estate office.

The railroad carried troops during World War I, so back then it was very busy, with hundreds of people out there at the station. In my time, you'd see rather modest crowds, unless there was a special event, or a special train; then there would be a lot more people waiting to board. People taking the train could arrive at the station by taking the Key System train that ran down 40th Street either from the Piedmont Station or from San Francisco, or perhaps the No. 6 line on Broadway, or they'd simply walk to the station. When the railroad was thriving, there were about twenty-five trains a day. Usually they were two-car passenger trains. At night they'd run two freight trains—one that went out north, and one that came in very early in the morning.

Convenient and Not Very Expensive

Some of the passenger cars were motorized, some were trailers. A motor could pull a trailer, which was not powered. They were older cars, very plain, and most of them built locally. Most of the motor cars were combinations, which meant that they included a baggage compartment up front. For a few years the Sacramento Northern ran parlor observation cars on express trains. The Meteor, which came all the way from Chico, was one; the Comet was another. Both served meals and were very comfortable. You couldn't smoke in the straight coaches—you'd have to go to the smoking section of the motor car. You could also smoke in the parlor cars.

There were two unique cars that were used exclusively on what they called the school train, which ran to Concord, where Contra Costa County's big high school

Sacramento Northern parlor car "Meteor," 40th and Shafter depot, circa 1935. *Ted Wurm Collection*

Advertisement, passenger car interior, 1936, Western Railway Museum

was located. They'd pick up kids, starting in Moraga Valley. It was a six-car train, so they had a pretty good load of kids. The school train would pick them up in the morning, then take them home in the afternoon. There was also a small, two-car school train that ran between San Francisco and St. Mary's College in Moraga.

The exteriors of the cars were painted dark green. The seats were upholstered in dark red mohair. Each car had a restroom and drinking fountain. On the express trains—the Comet and Meteor—there were white linen coverings for the tops of the seats. The windows were operable, thank God, because in the valley it would get terribly hot. The windows had bars across them to prevent anyone from sticking their arm out. The lighting was fine—good enough to read by at night.

Sacramento Northern car interior, 1940. *Ted Wurm Collection*

The Sacramento Northern ran both local and express trains. A lot of the service was commute traffic to San Francisco. People would board as far out as Concord, Lafayette, Walnut Creek, or closer in at Montclair or Temescal. It was an easy commute and competitively priced. Other folks would take the train to intermediate points to visit friends or relatives, or even to vacation.

People would also take the train to Sacramento. It was convenient and not very expensive. On Sundays they offered the whole roundtrip for one dollar! The one-way trip took a little over two hours, which was slightly slower than the Southern Pacific, which skirted the hills by going through Richmond and Martinez. The Sacramento Northern crossed the Sacramento River by ferry. Loading the train, taking it across to the other side, and unloading it all took time. The Southern Pacific, too, had had a ferry, but they had more money, so they eventually built a bridge at Benicia.

The Oakland Bay Bridge was completed at the end of 1936. In early 1939, after the Sacramento Northern got their train control equipment installed, they were allowed to cross the Bay Bridge on the rails into San Francisco to the Bay Bridge terminal. I was fortunate enough to have ridden the very first Sacramento Northern train that crossed the bridge into San Francisco.

On the passenger trains, the crew would consist of a motorman, a conductor, and one or two brakemen. All the employees were union. One of things that made it tough for the railroads to compete was that they had minimum crew laws.

Oscar Schindler, motorman, inside cab of Sacramento Northern locomotive #604, 40th and Shafter, 1941. *Photo: Paul Smith*

40th Street at Opal (looking westerly), 1912. *Photo: Cook; Vernon J. Sappers Collection*

40th Street at Opal (looking westerly), 2005.

Shafter at 45th Street (looking north), 1939. *Photo: Ted Wurm; Courtesy of Paul Smith*

Shafter at 45th Street (looking north), 2005.

Shafter at 41st Street (looking northerly), circa 1940. *Photo: Paul Smith*

Shafter at 41st Street (looking northerly), 2005.

Shafter at 42nd Street (looking south), circa 1940. *Photo: Paul Smith*

Shafter at 42nd Street (looking south), 2005.

The "Free" Highways

During the earlier years, automobile travel was not convenient. The roads weren't very good, and neither were the vehicles. So people took the train. What killed the railroads and took the passengers away was the automobile and the "free" highways that people could travel on—door to door.

Passenger service in and out of Oakland was discontinued in 1941. For a long time after passenger service ended, the Sacramento Northern ran electric powered freight trains. In the late 1940s they started making the switch to diesel engines, which were more economical to run. Finally, in 1957, all freight service in and out of Oakland was discontinued.

The railway was financially successful early on, when it was still the Oakland, Antioch and Eastern—or the San Francisco Sacramento Railroad. But it never was a big money maker. The main reason why it kept going was that the Public Utilities Commission wouldn't let them stop.

When it finally ended, they tore up the tracks on Shafter and repaved the street. Part of the right-of-way along Lake Temescal was used by the new Highway 13.

As a culture, we got fascinated with freeways and built them like they were going out of style. Everything became oriented toward automobile transportation. Now they're finding that it isn't the greatest thing in the world. We see light rail systems being built again and surviving, like in San Jose, Sacramento, Portland, and Seattle. Of course in Europe, rail has remained *the* way to go. It's very efficient. So I think interurban rail transportation probably will be revived.

I just took the train up to Corvallis to visit my daughter. I picked up the train—Amtrak—in Emeryville. It's a very, very comfortable way to go. It's a little expensive now, but if you can afford it, it's great. ✦

Detail, exterior of streetcar, Western Railway Museum, 2005.

Background: Sacramento Northern car 1020, Western Railway Museum, 2005.

Sacramento Northern, departing station at Shafter and 40th Street (looking south), circa 1940.
Photo: Paul Smith

Shafter at 41st Sreet (looking northerly), circa 1940. *Photo: Paul Smith*

Shafter and 40th Street
(looking south), 2005.

Shafter at 41st Sreet (looking northerly), 2006.

RATES OF PAY

Rule 84. Basic hourly rates of pay applicable to the employes and the work coming within the scope of this agreement shall be as follows:

Rule Section			*Hourly Rate*
51		Machinists	$ .77
52		Machinist Helpers	.51
54		Blacksmiths	.77
55		Blacksmith Helpers	.51
60		Sheet Metal Workers	.77
61		Sheet Metal Worker Helpers	.51
63	(a)	Electricians	.77
63	(b)	Electrical Inspectors	.68
65		Electrical Worker Helpers	.51
69	(a)	Passenger Carmen	.77
69	(b)	Passenger Carmen	[illegible]
70	(a)	Freight Carmen	[illegible]
70	(b)	Freight Carmen	[illegible]
71		Car Inspectors	[illegible]
72		Carmen Helpers	[illegible]
73	(a)	Painters	.77
73	(b)	Painters	.65
74		Painter Helpers	.51
82		Coach Cleaners	.41

SACRAMENTO NORTHERN RAILWAY No. 2517
1933
PASS Carlo Avanzino---
Car Cleaner,
Sacramento Northern Railway.
OVER ENTIRE SYSTEM UNTIL DECEMBER 31, 1933, UNLESS OTHERWISE ORDERED OR SPECIFIED SUBJECT TO CONDITIONS ON BACK. VALID WHEN COUNTERSIGNED BY M. F. ZIEHN OR W. E.
COUNTERSIGNED

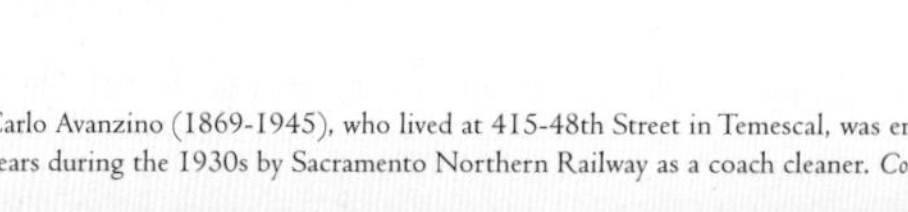

Carlo Avanzino (1869-1945), who lived at 415-48th Street in Temescal, was employed for several years during the 1930s by Sacramento Northern Railway as a coach cleaner. *Courtesy of Ron Avanzino*

Don Olsen

Born in 1923, Don Olsen remembers that, as a child growing up in Minneapolis, he saw, "plumes of smoke all over, even on Sunday. Practically everybody had an Uncle Jim who was an engineer or motorman or conductor." A dream of Don's had been to work on a railroad someday, and after serving in World War II and a couple of years studying engineering at UC Berkeley, he spent two happy years working as a fireman on the Southern Pacific out of Dunsmuir in northern California. His interest in trains continued throughout his long career as an air pollution control engineer, so that by the time he retired in 1975, he had more than 40,000 feet of 16 mm film about trains, most of which he himself had shot. With this footage, and more that he acquired from other rail fans, Don launched his second career as a writer, editor, and producer of train videos, under the name of Catenary Films. From his apartment in Walnut Creek, Don currently is working on his 21st video.

The Interurbans Were Wonderful

It's been said that, as an industry, interurbans had the briefest rise and fall of any. They spread like wildfire. Most interurban railroads in this country were built beginning in the 1890s, when electric propulsion became practical. The big railroads already were there, but they didn't serve every little hamlet along the way. That's why the interurbans were so popular. People could hop on and go a few miles to the next little town to shop at the market. In the beginning, practically everybody used them. In a lot of these little towns, the roads were horrible, so even those who had automobiles still had to hitch up a horse and buggy. The interurbans were wonderful; they ran frequently, and fares were relatively reasonable. It wasn't only townsfolk who took them—farmers shipped their produce. It's hard for us to imagine it, but around the turn of the century, train time at the small town depot was a big event. Everything came by railroad. It was part of the warp and woof of existence.

On the other hand, many of the interurbans, including some local ones, were just arms of real estate ventures. You could take empty land, run a streetcar line out to it, and property would immediately rise in value. That's the way many early suburbs got started. Other interurbans were just developers' dreams for which there never was any sound basis. Much of the impetus to build the original Oakland, Antioch and Eastern Railway—the predecessor to the Sacramento Northern—was tied to this kind of real

Realty Syndicate Plans Selling Campaign in Vicinity of Terminal of New Railroad

An aggressive selling campaign affecting property along the route and at the terminus of the Oakland and Antioch railway is being planned by Sales Manager C. V. King of the Realty Syndicate. The company is now extending its rails out Shafter avenue and are well along east of College avenue.

About thirty lots on Fortieth street between Telegraph avenue and Opal street will be materially enhanced in value by the operation of the road and the establishment of the terminus and transfer point at Fortieth and Shafter avenue.

"In my opinion," said Manager King yesterday, "Fortieth street will rapidly develop into a new business street and investors may expect a substantial increase in value by July 1st next when trains of the Oakland and Antioch will be in operation. We have a number of scattered lots along Shafter avenue that are being eagerly sought by speculators and with continued activity along Fortieth street, the sales department is kept busy.

Oakland Enquirer
October 21, 1911

Map (detail) of Oakland, 1900. Dark areas indicate land owned by the Realty Syndicate. At the center of the circle is the site chosen in 1911 for the Oakland, Antioch and Easter depot. *Map by William J. Dingee; Courtesy of the Oakland History Room*

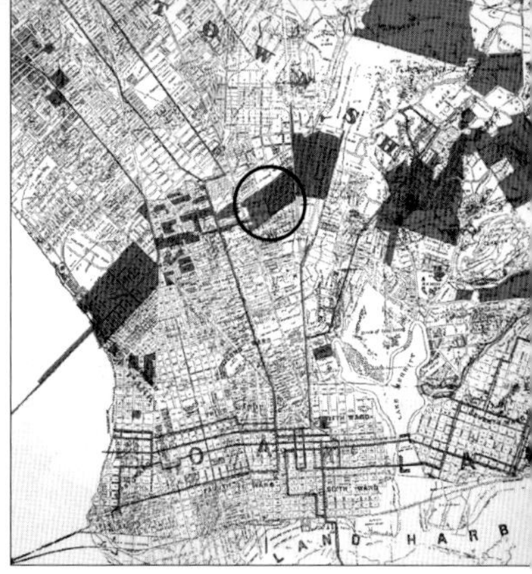

estate speculation. In the early 1900s, most of the land east of the hills was just open country. The hope of significant development in Contra Costa County never really materialized, at least, not until after the Sacramento Northern was gone. Still, the railroad enjoyed a relative amount of success in the beginning because they served areas where there wasn't any other rail transportation.

The Grade Up Shafter

Until 1939, the Sacramento Northern had an arrangement with the Key System which allowed them to run over Key System trackage down to the Key pier, where passengers could catch ferries to San Francisco. In 1939 the Sacramento Northern was able to run trains on the lower deck of the Bay Bridge, which had opened only a couple years earlier. This was after they'd installed the required additional safety devices to help ensure that there wouldn't be any collisions. Key System trains and Southern Pacific electrics were also running on the bridge at this point.

Tillio and Elvira Avanzino at 409-48th Street, with RR crossing sign on Shafter in background, circa 1923. *Courtesy of Ron Avanzino*

The grade up Shafter was very heavy, and coming in and out of the hills the curves were quite sharp. On the east side of the tunnel, the track went into Redwood Canyon. From there, it went to Moraga and through Lafayette, Walnut Creek, and Concord to Port Chicago. From there it turned east. Originally, they were going to go as far east as Antioch, but they never made it. At a junction called West Pittsburg, the line turned north and crossed the Sacramento River on a unique, cat-

Ferry "Ramon" crossing Carquinez Straight near West Pittsburg, carrying Sacramento Northern train, circa 1950. *Ted Wurm Collection*

enary-equipped ferry [having overhead electrified wire] that allowed trains to run on and off the ferry under their own power. The route continued north, passing Rio Vista Junction, and on to Sacramento. From Sacramento, they just kept going north until they got to Chico. Altogether it was a little over 180 miles, making it one of the longest electric interurban railroads in the county.

Thumping and Bumping

By the time I visited the station at Shafter and 40th Street, there no longer was passenger service. Even so, the whole operation there was terribly inefficient, because there was so little space. They'd have to haul a car out here and tuck it back in over there. They did amazingly well considering the shortcomings of that little station.

There was a big freight shed facing Shafter. As time went by, something that declined—on all railroads, actually—was what they call LCL, which stands for "less than car load." Trucks would back up to the freight shed on the 40th Street side and unload maybe a few boxes, or some express, which would then be stored in the shed. From there it would be transferred to freight cars on the other side of the shed. There was a time when that was very busy. Ultimately, that proved to be very inefficient. Trucks just took it all away. If you're going to put it on a truck in the first place, why bother to transload it to a box car on one end and put it back on a truck on the other end? As time went on, the freight shed was used less and less.

There was a set of tracks in the yard that branched off to the east from Shafter and connected with the Key System tracks on 40th Street. This allowed them to turn equipment around without needing to have a loop. They could run cars out heading in the direction of Broadway, go backwards down 40th, and come back up Shafter facing the other way. When they were making up trains, sometimes they'd also go out onto 40th because there just wasn't room in the yard. They did a lot of that on Shafter, too, and, of course, the thumping and bumping of cars coming together caused a lot of noise.

Sacramento Northern engine and caboose, 41st and Shafter, 1940. *Photo: Paul Smith*

Same view, from Thunder Road Treatment Center, 41st and Shafter, 2005.

Charles "Chas" Bowman, freight conductor, inside caboose, 40th and Shafter, circa 1940. *Photo: Paul Smith*

Given that passenger service had been abandoned before I got there, I was fortunate to have been able to ride a freight from Oakland to Sacramento. At the time, there was a kind of post-war boom, which most railroads shared. It was 1949, and they were still very busy with freight. My old buddy Vernon Sappers knew practically every crewman on the railroad. He went to a conductor whom he knew and made the arrangements. All I had to do was to be there at a given hour—I think the train left Oakland at eight or nine in the morning. They had a trainmaster there by the name of Long, who was not at all sympathetic to this kind of thing. Before we left, the conductor explained to me that as we pulled out I would have to get down on the floor of the caboose so that Mr. Long wouldn't see me. Once we got a little ways up Shafter, I could sit up in the cupola. It was an all-day journey to Sacramento, because of all the switching along the way.

Big, Heavy, Powerful Cars

In 1927, the Western Pacific bought the Sacramento Northern primarily to use as a freight feeder. There weren't a lot of local destinations on the Sacramento Northern line for carloads of produce or freight. But somebody, from Orland, for instance, might want a carload of manufactured goods from New York. It would come out to whatever point on the Western Pacific that had a connection on the Sacramento Northern, then the Sacramento Northern would take that car to the local purchaser. In the same way, when fruit or vegetables were ready for market, the Sacramento Northern hauled a lot of refrigerator cars, which would then hook up with the Western Pacific.

The Sacramento Northern also was a co-owner, together with the Key System, of the Oakland Terminal Railway. When the Sacramento Northern brought freight trains down Shafter to the yard at 40th Street, the Oakland Terminal Railway would take over and haul them down to the Oakland waterfront where stuff would be trans-shipped.

Shafter, (looking north toward 42nd Street), circa 1920. *Courtesy of Paul Smith*

Shafter, (looking north toward 42nd Street), 2005.

And, of course, it worked in the other direction too. So, in most respects, the Sacramento Northern freight service was just like the regular railroad; they'd haul about everything and anything.

Most of the Sacramento Northern cars were built in the early teens. They were big, heavy, powerful cars. The trains could do sixty, seventy miles an hour when they were out in open country. Most of the through trains—the north-south trains—were two or three cars long, except in the off-hours. The thing that originally made electric railroading practical, once the technical aspects were perfected, was the flexibility. It was very easy to couple up as many cars as you needed for a run.

After 1929 when they established through service, the Sacramento Northern ran first class trains. The Meteor, the Comet, the Sacramento Limited—there were quite a number of them—carried a parlor car that eventually was equipped with a little galley so they could serve refreshments. Originally they charged an extra twenty-five cents to sit in a parlor car. In those days that was a lot—more than many people could afford.

The equipment remained pretty basic, and as the years went by it became outmoded. I've seen drawings of streamlined designs intended to improve and modernize service, but there was never the money to do it. They kept the old equipment, they maintained it well, and it was safe. But it probably had a negative effect as far as the public went when other railroads, beginning in the early 1930s, started streamlining. That obviously caught the public's imagination. Very few interurbans could afford to do that, however, and it probably just added to the image in the public's mind that interurbans were passé.

Anti-Railroad Sentiment

In the beginning, electric railroads had a kind of cachet. People thought, "Hey, we've got an electric railroad. Boy, we're really getting up in the world!" If you look at some of the early photographs of East Bay cities, back when the Southern Pacific was first electrifying their commuter lines, you can see that there was a house here, one up on a hill over there. Eventually, of course, as more and more people arrived, the area became settled, and there began to be this anti-railroad sentiment. People stopped being happy about having these trains rumbling by.

Locating the station at 40th Street and Shafter was not a very good choice, but

Background: caboose, Sacramento Northern rail yard, 41st and Shafter, circa 1940. *Photo: Paul Smith*

Council Studies Protest on Trains on Shafter Avenue

Halting Western Pacific Railroad freight shipments over Sacramento Northern Railroad tracks on Shafter avenue was advocated at last night's Oakland City Council meeting by James M. Leaver of the Rockridge Improvement Club.

John B. Rosson, attorney for the rail lines, explained that an application for a franchise to operate trains on Union street had been before the council for more than a year.

"If the council would grant our request for a track on Union street we would not have to use the Shafter avenue route," Rosson told the council. . . .

Permission to use the Union street route had been delayed because of protests from the West Oakland area and because trains would have to cross the eventual extension of the East Shore Freeway. . . .

Leaver said the railroad operation on Shafter avenue, which is in a residential neighborhood and passes five schools, is retarding development of that section of North Oakland.

Oakland Post-Enquirer
July 11, 1947

. . . Said Mrs. Ernest Porter, 5264 Shafter, "Get them out as fast as possible; the vibrations have been shaking my pictures askew for years!"

The Montclarion
July 31, 1947

maybe that was the only option at the time. They were so cramped! Somebody, I presume, was able to get the easement to lay track on Shafter, which the residents came to really hate. The single track was laid off-center, anticipating that they might have double tracks eventually. Well, that never happened. The track, which ran on the west side of Shafter, was close enough to the curb so that there was barely room for a car to be parked there. There were a lot of incidents when cars weren't carefully parked. They'd have to stop the train, and the trainman would have to ring doorbells to get somebody to move their car. Or they'd try to squeeze by, which sometimes meant that somebody would get their fender torn off. These incidents were all relatively minor, but it didn't help the situation. The trains always ran very slowly when they were on city streets, but it was an operational headache.

Over the years, as they lived with these trains rumbling along Shafter twenty-four hours a day, many residents tried to get the city council to limit the number of trains and the times when they could run. They also fought to get rid of the tracks altogether. Following World War II, the Sacramento Northern's franchise expired, and they ran for years, you might say, on a day-to-day basis. The city council technically could have shut them down. They never did formally extend the franchise to operate on Shafter, even though it wasn't until 1957 that the last freight ran out of Oakland.

Vacant Sacramento Northern shops, 40th and Shafter (looking west), 1957. *Courtesy of the Oakland History Room*

Downfall

It had been pretty expensive to build the Sacramento Northern in the first place, which saddled the company with debt right from the beginning. But its downfall really came once automobiles were available in quantities and farmers had their pick-up trucks to get their produce to market or milk to the dairy, and roads got better. Also, not too many interurbans survived the Depression; of those that did, almost all were gone by World War II.

Rail yard, 41st and Shafter (looking southerly), 1957. *Ted Wurm Collection*

The Sacramento Northern abandoned passenger service out of Oakland in 1941. It's curious that so many electric railroads all over the country were abandoned in 1940, 1941—it's almost as if the railroads knew there was a war coming, and that if they didn't get rid of their passenger service, they'd be forced to keep it going during the war.

What kept the Sacramento Northern alive much longer than so many other interurbans was that Western Pacific continued to use the Sacramento Northern as a freight feeder. As passenger revenues kept dropping, it was the freight that kept them alive. That lasted well through the war. In the early 1950s, the Korean War made them busy again. A lot of shipments were open flatcars with war materiel on them, such as tanks and trucks. The last Sacramento Northern freight out of Oakland was on February 28, 1957.

Demolished Sacramento Northern shops, 40th and Shafter (looking west), 1957. *Courtesy of John Harder*

Oakland chamber of commerce last week requested the city council to consider a plan to acquire the rights-of-way of Sacramento-Northern for use of its tunnel connecting Alameda and Contra Costa counties. . . .

Along with this second tunnel would be the extension of Park blvd. up Shepherd canyon, opening a vast new acreage for home development in the hills.

The Montclarion
November 20, 1947

It is generally agreed that some form of rapid transit must be seriously considered as a key ultimate method of coping with the problem of getting many hundreds of Central Contra Costa commuters to and from work speedily and conveniently.

In that connection, the possibility of using the old Sacramento Northern Railroad tracks for resumption of passenger commute service is a subject of utmost importance.

Lafayette Sun
August 6, 1954

Harry A. Mitchell, former president of Sacramento Northern and of Western Pacific, and now a trustee in bankruptcy for SN, says he doesn't believe there is much likelihood of future use of the SN tracks for resumption of commute service. . . .

A rapid transit survey is now under way by the San Francisco Bay Area Rapid Transit Commission. (Incidentally, Mitchell is chairman of the commission.)

Lafayette Sun
September 10, 1954

Background: crossing sign (not original), Canyon, 2005.

Ceremony announcing scheduled completion of the Oakland Civic Center Hospital, east side of Shafter at 40th Street, 1959. *Courtesy of Thunder Road Treatment Center*

It's All Overgrown

At the west entrance to the tunnel, at the head of Shepherd Canyon, the former Sacramento Northern right-of-way has been so thoroughly obliterated that you'd never know a railroad had been there. There are houses now sitting where the railroad went through a cut, before it went into the tunnel. There was a little stop called Havens, a short ways down from there, and that's also totally gone.

If you drive the road that goes up over the hills and comes down the other side, there's a place where you can still see a railing. The road crossed the mouth of the tunnel right there. If you look down, you can see that something had been there; but, again, it's all overgrown. For years you could see a wider spot on the right-of-way where the maintenance buildings and a substation had been, but it's no longer evident.

In Redwood Canyon, essentially nothing happened to the right-of-way. They just tore up the track. Although it's become heavily overgrown, you can still see where the tunnel mouth and some of the places where the right-of-way had been. Nobody built on it, because it belongs to the East Bay Municipal Utilities District watershed. It's pristine today, just like it was then, when the Sacramento Northern stopped at the couple of picnic areas that they maintained. If you continue on down toward the little hamlet of Canyon, you can see an embankment. The bridges themselves are gone, but you can see where the railroad crossed over the road.

"Short Line," Lake Temescal (looking northerly). *Photo: Estey; Vernon J. Sappers Collection*

Bike path, on former right-of-way, Lake Temescal (looking northerly).

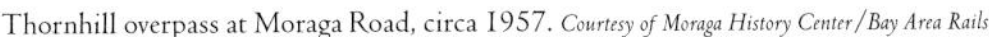

Thornhill overpass at Moraga Road, circa 1957. *Courtesy of Moraga History Center/Bay Area Rails*

Thornhill at Moraga Road, 2006.

When you get out past Moraga, near St. Mary's College, a lot of the former right-of-way is now a hiking trail. You can literally walk the right-of-way on a trail through Lafayette to Walnut Creek, though it's all been tremendously developed. After you leave Walnut Creek, as you go north on 680 toward Concord, the BART tracks use several miles of what had been the Sacramento Northern right-of-way.

Part of the Web

For somebody of my age, there was a kind of aura that surrounded the industry as a whole. Many people worked for railroads, and it was very much a part of the web of our social structure. Now, the automobile has become not only ascendant, but completely dominant. Even if some of these modes of transportation like the Sacramento Northern still existed, people probably wouldn't use them, because they're too married to their cars. When the interurbans developed, there wasn't any alternative, and people welcomed them with open arms. Now, it's hard to get people off the highways to commute by bus or rail. People just don't want to leave their cars. They're too convenient. ✦

Detail, exterior of streetcar, Western Railway Museum, 2005.

Contra Costa county benefited considerably from the railroad, although possibly not as much as was expected. While it was a definite benefit to the farmers along the route, from a real estate standpoint the railroad did not cause nearly the change in Contra Costa that was caused by the low level [Caldecott] highway tunnel.

The Montclarion
July 1, 1948

Intersection of 41st and Shafter (looking southerly), and abandonned Sacramento Northern rail yard 1957. *Courtesy of John Harder*

Background: Preparation of site for "Temescal Station," a 30-unit condo and townhouse development, 40th and Shafter (looking west), 2005.

A railroad operates at a cost of about $1.50 per mile, as against 40 cents per mile for buses. The wide difference is due mainly to maintenance of the roadbed. Railroad upkeep is by the company; upkeep of the roads traveled by buses is paid for by taxes.

Oakland Tribune
April 25, 1957

Intersection of 41st and Shafter (looking southerly), 2005.

On motion of Councilman Vernon Lantz, . . . the council voted unanimously yesterday to confer with officials of railroad firms and the Port of Oakland in an effort to reroute Western Pacific freight trains into the port area. . . .

Lantz pointed out that removal of Western Pacific tracks from Shafter Avenue would permit that street to be used as the route for the proposed new freeway into Contra Costa County.

Oakland Tribune
September 24, 1947

Grove-Shafter Freeway

The Politics and Consequences of Choosing a Route

46th Street deadend at Highway 24 (looking east), 2005.

Introduction

In 1957, at the very moment when many Temescal and Rockridge neighbors were celebrating the end of their long battle to remove the Sacramento Northern tracks from Shafter Avenue, another issue, potentially far more disruptive to North Oakland, was brewing: the coming of the Grove-Shafter Freeway. What is now the combined Highway I-980/24 stretch that extends from I-880 to the Caldecott Tunnel, the Grove-Shafter Freeway (named for the two primary adjacent streets it paralleled) had been on the state's Division of Highway's drawing board since the 1940s. It was not until the fall of 1955, however, when word spread of a proposal to widen 51st Street to turn it into a major connector between Moraga Avenue and the proposed Grove-Shafter Freeway, that many North Oaklanders caught wind of the plan.

A public meeting convened by the state at Oakland Technical High School in December 1956, where numerous possible routes for the freeway were presented, only raised people's apprehensions about the freeway's impact on the neighborhood. Raymond Mellana and Sewall Glinternick, whose firsthand accounts follow, convey what many in Temescal and Rockridge feared. They also describe the community's and their own determination to have a say in the decisions that seemingly were being handed down from Sacramento and Oakland City Hall. It is arguable just how effective local efforts were in influencing the final outcome; for both Ray and Sewall, even the victories they could point to were at best bittersweet.

In a kind of irony that hindsight often reveals, concerns about safety, nuisance, and lowered property values that were eliminated in 1957 with the shutting down of the Sacramento Northern merely resurfaced in 1969 when the first phase of the Grove-Shafter opened. Although the area of Temescal immediately impacted shifted by a few blocks, neighbors now had to deal with air and sound pollution, forbidding freeway overpasses, residential streets that dead-ended, litter, and lowered property values. Unlike the Sacramento Northern, however, the freeway also decimated entire commercial districts, such as on Grove Street and at Telegraph and 55th. When we compound the loss of many long-established, neighborhood-serving businesses with the hundreds of families who moved away when their homes were

Sign, 41st Street and Dover, at freeway, 2005.

taken for the freeway right-of-way, it is not hard to see why residential and commercial areas near the freeway fell into decline during the 1970s and 1980s. In many places, revival remains elusive.

Another irony is that where the community effort in the 1940s and 1950s was to remove Sacramento Northern trains from Shafter, the building of the Grove-Shafter Freeway physically removed a portion of Shafter Avenue itself. Today, the stretch of Shafter that once continued above College Avenue to Chabot Road lies beneath the freeway and BART. Thus, in a very literal sense, the end of one form of transportation paved the way for another.

College Avenue (looking east), with the freeway and Rockridge BART station under construction, 1967. *Courtesy of the Oakland Cultural Heritage Survey*

The greatest beneficiaries of the new freeway (aside from the building trades and real estate industry) were to be those commuting through the Caldecott Tunnel, whose third bore had been completed in 1964. The Grove-Shafter promised to be much faster than the old, congested route along Tunnel Road and upper Broadway. This benefit was part of the regional view held by the Division of Highways whose focus was more on California's mushrooming suburban populations than on older urban communities (and whose incentives included major federal funding for highway projects). Despite the loss to the neighborhood that the Grove-Shafter Freeway represented for many in North Oakland, locals were not insensitive to this larger need. When BART in the late 1950s proposed building a portion of its Concord line down the middle of sections of the new freeway, many in Temescal and Rockridge saw that as an important public benefit.

Meanwhile, even with BART and the intermittent widening of Highway 24 that has taken place since the first segment opened in 1969, freeway congestion has persisted. Caltrans' current plan, despite an organized protest from the North Oakland community, is to add a fourth bore to the Caldecott Tunnel. Perhaps this is the ultimate, sad irony. As Sewall says, "What appears to be a nifty solution turns out to be a horror story. We try to keep pace by increasing the number of freeways, or number of lanes, but we can't do it."

Public meeting, sponsored by Caltrans and held at Chabot Middle School, to discuss plans for a fourth bore of the Caldecott Tunnel, June 15, 2006.

46th Street and Grove (looking west), during construction of the Grove-Shafter Freeway and BART, circa 1967. *Courtesy of the Oakland Cultural Heritage Survey*

Raymond Mellana

Ray Mellana is a product of Temescal. Born into the predominantly Italian neighborhood in 1919, and having grown up and then worked in it until his retirement, he's been intimately familiar with Temescal's sights, sounds, and smells. It was Ray's familiarity and his love of Temescal's traditional, vibrant community that informed his role in the debate that surfaced in the late 1950s over what has been one of Temescal's most divisive issues as a community: the routing of the Grove-Shafter Freeway through North Oakland.

Unlike his father, Ray was not cut out to be a grocer. "I couldn't stand arguing over the price of goods with ladies squeezing tomatoes," Ray recalls with a laugh. Born and raised in the seven-room flat over his parents' grocery store on the corner of Grove and 46th Street in Temescal, Ray eventually chose law as his profession. "I was the only son to go to college of any of the five brothers who'd come over from Italy."

Ray graduated from UC Berkeley in 1940. A year later, after he had completed one year at Boalt Law School, the United States entered the Second World War and Ray was drafted into the army. When the war ended, Ray returned to law school. In 1948, married, with a young daughter, and a law degree in hand, he went looking for a job. "I knocked on most of the doors of the Italian lawyers practicing in downtown Oakland—some of them knew my family because of Mom and Dad's store in Temescal. But nothing turned up."

That's when William Ghiglieri, manager of the Temescal branch of the Bank of America, told Ray about a lawyer across the street, Aldo Guidotti, whose office at 4918 Telegraph was above Pete Tira's furniture store. Ray went to talk with Aldo, and they hit it off. Except for five years when Ray served as a deputy district attorney for Alameda County, Ray and Aldo were partners until Ray retired in 1988. "Aldo and I became good friends, never having had a dispute in over thirty years of practice." For a good many of those years, theirs was the only law office in Temescal.

"It was a general practice that was built on clients coming in off the street—often without an appointment—who were willing to climb the twenty-two steps to the office above the furniture store. Often my fee would be in the form of a box of raviolis—and the fee was welcome! Aldo and I wrote a lot of ten-dollar wills. Frankly, we couldn't have overcharged, because we were in a community of hard, tight-fisted Italians who knew how to bargain for services."

Like Aldo in the early years of his law practice, Ray threw himself into civic affairs, serving in leadership positions in many community organizations. While president of the Temescal Merchants Association in the late 1950s, Ray found himself at the center of a political storm when news surfaced that the California State Highway Division was planning to build a freeway through the Temescal and Rockridge districts of North Oakland. As the debate about the proposed freeway escalated, the Citizens Committee

Against the Grove-Shafter Freeway was formed, and Ray became its legal advisor and spokesman.

In 1960, with that debate still raging, Aldo and Ray moved their offices from above the furniture store on Telegraph into what they officially named the Temescal Law Building, at 4895 Shattuck (demolished in 2005). Over the years, Ray raised five children—four daughters from his first marriage, to Helen, who died in 1955, and a son with his second wife, also now deceased. When Ray remarried in 1966, he and his new wife, Diana, moved to Orinda and into a home large enough to accommodate all the children—and Ray's parents who eventually came to live with them. As Ray approached retirement, he and Diana moved to the Sierra foothill community of Sonora, where they make their home today.

A Close-Knit Community

My dad, Peter Mellana, was about seventeen when he emigrated to America from the Piemonte region in northern Italy. The earthquake and fire of 1906 brought my parents from San Francisco to Oakland. Dad, I think, had been courting my mother, Mary Coggiola, at the time. My mother's family moved into a house on McElroy Street in West Oakland. My dad established a partnership with Eddie Cassina and opened a grocery store on Peralta Street not far from McElroy. My mom got a job rolling cigars in a factory in West Oakland and then later worked in a laundry there.

My parents married in 1912. At some point they purchased from my Aunt Mary a grocery business on Grove near the corner of 46th Street, and lived in the rear of the store. The building was owned by the Sweeney sisters, who were *very* Irish—they both spoke with an Irish brogue. My parents subsequently bought the building next door on the corner, at 4539 Grove, and had it elevated and a store built on the ground floor. That was the building in which I and my younger sister, Hazel, were born and raised.

4539 Grove Street, 1938. *Courtesy of Ray Mellana*

4539 Martin Luther King Jr. Way, 2004.

The thing I liked best about the house was the cellar, where Dad made his wine. In those days, the law allowed families to make 50 gallons or so of wine for their own consumption. There was a chap named Fiorentino Aletto, who made his own crushers and pressers and rented them out to all the Italians in Temescal. Dad would rent a crusher, and then he and I would go down to the Santa Fe tracks in Emeryville where the grapes were brought in. We'd load up Dad's Model T truck and bring the grapes home. I used to love to watch my dad crush the grapes. In all of Temescal, in all the homes, people were making wine—the fumes! September and October were the best months of the year because that was all you smelled.

My parents were part of a close-knit community that spoke Italian almost exclusively—on the streets and in the stores, and in their own store. Around 1942, my parents sold the store to Mr. Bernardi, who used to peddle fruits and vegetables from his truck all through Temescal. They bought a lot off Broadway Terrace and built a home—their first house in thirty years as a married couple where they were able to have a garden.

We Never Crossed Grove

My sense of the Temescal neighborhood at the time was that it was bounded on the south by 39th Street, or perhaps MacArthur Boulevard—which used to be called Mosswood Avenue, then Broadway on the east, and westward to the Emeryville line, almost to San Pablo. On the north side, it extended up to 55th Street, then over to College and around to Broadway where the Rockridge Shopping Center is now. The real core of Temescal was between 40th and 55th Street along Telegraph, and between Grove and Broadway.

There weren't a lot of kids in the neighborhood in those days, maybe a dozen in the two-block area from Grove to Market. During the Depression years, the Italians didn't have large families; the average was two or three kids. At the time, there was substantial traffic on Grove because of the No. 3 streetcar. We never crossed Grove because our folks just didn't want us crossing those busy streets. For the same reason, I didn't go to Emerson Elementary, which was on the east side of Telegraph. Instead, I went to Santa Fe Elementary on Market Street. My mother and father never let me have a bicycle, because it was too dangerous on those heavily trafficked streets of Temescal!

> **Not too many years ago the standing joke was that the only safe way to cross Telegraph Avenue was to be born on the other side.**
>
> *The Oakland Telegraph*
> October 30, 1959

Later I went to Woodrow Wilson Junior High [renamed Carter Middle School], which was across Telegraph on 48th Street. I chose to go to Oakland Tech for high school because that was where most of my buddies on the street went, particularly our hero, Cookie Lavagetto, the professional ball player, who had lived right across from me on 46th Street. Oakland Tech at that time was integrated, particularly with Asians from Chinatown, Japanese, and some blacks. But it was predominantly Italian, Irish, and a mix of other European heritages.

There was a substantial group of Irish in the neighborhood, some Hispanic—not many—say from 47th Street down to 40th. There was only one black family on 46th Street—Mr. and Mrs. Clark, a nice couple. Their home was beautiful. Mr. Clark was a porter for the Southern Pacific Railroad.

4629 Grove Street/MLK (looking west), formerly the Pullman Laundry.

The Pullman company had a laundry on Grove at 47th Street, just a block from my folks' grocery, where they laundered linen from the Pullman cars. It was a big operation that had a whistle that sounded at noon and at closing time. Directly across from that was the Snow Laundry. Employees from both laundries would come to my dad's grocery for their lunch sandwiches.

We felt safe there because we knew our neighbors, people who had been there for fifteen, twenty years. These were people who had roots in the neighborhood, and many stayed there until they died.

Through the Heart of Temescal

East entrance of the Kennedy, or "Old" Tunnel, circa 1925. *Courtesy of the Oakland History Room*

I remember Mom and Dad taking us for rides into Contra Costa, to visit friends or relatives—it was all farmland in the early 1920s. Halfway up Tunnel Road we'd have to stop the 1923 Buick because it was huffing and puffing and the radiator was boiling over. We'd have to refill the radiator and wait for it to get its breath back before getting into the old tunnel. It wasn't until 1937 that the Broadway Low-Level Tunnel [renamed the Caldecott] first opened. For many years it was just the two bores. A third bore was added when they were building the freeway in the 1960s.

I first heard about the proposed Grove-Shafter Freeway in the late 1950s in one of the local newspapers, either the *Oakland Tribune* or the *Oakland Telegraph,* which was a weekly newspaper published by Sewall Glinternick. He mostly included stories that were of immediate neighborhood interest.

Sewall was one of the early active opponents of the freeway proposal, because, according to the early plans shown by the California Highway Division—that's what it was called before it was renamed Caltrans—it was to cut right through the heart of Temescal and a good part of Rockridge. The route would have come up from the Bay Bridge through the lower part of West Oakland, across West Street and Grove, taking the middle part of 46th Street, and up across Shattuck. The freeway would have passed at a diagonal across Telegraph Avenue, so that the space required, not only for the highway but for the adjacent service area, would have taken a lot of the properties on both sides of Telegraph. It would have taken out Pete Tira's furniture store where we had our law office and the bank next door at the corner of 49th and Telegraph. It would have pretty well demolished most of the buildings in Temescal's central business district.

Our principal objection to the proposal—and we found out about this from hearings and some digging that Sewall and others did—was that the Cal Highway Division also had plans that routed the freeway out of the Caldecott Tunnel and down Ashby Avenue in a straight line all the way to the East Shore Freeway [now Interstate 80]. It was a clean cut, right down an existing street. Of course they would wipe out a lot of residences and some businesses on Ashby as well, though it was principally residential all the way down.

But then the state said, "Ah! We can build BART and have the tracks run down the middle of the freeway, or along side it. This apparently caused them to switch from their original Ashby Avenue route to one that cut toward downtown Oakland, and this new plan was eventually sold to most of the Oakland city councilmen.

The College Avenue merchants and the Temescal merchants, as well as some Piedmont Avenue merchants, joined forces and began to vocally oppose the plan by writing letters, attending city council meetings, and talking to city councilmen and members of the Alameda County Board of

A new low in public relations was achieved with the December 19 [1956] hearing. The engineers advertised the meeting as a "hearing designed to acquaint local officials and interested individuals with information which had been devloped in connection with the planning of this freeway."

North Oaklanders had been asking for such information for almost a year, and had been refused it. They assumed that everyone else had also been refused this information. At the hearing they found out how wrong they were. After the engineers had delivered what amounted to a sales pitch for the proposed route, representatives of the Chamber of Commerce and various downtown groups read prepared statements and presented resolutions favoring the state's plan. It was apparent to even the dullest person present that the state had consulted with various groups—while they were carefully keeping the people in the area affected completely in the dark. Instead of creating support for their plan, the engineers had succeeded—through the poorest sort of public relations—in alienating an entire section of Oakland.

Dean Waring
Claremont Press
July 8, 1960

Three years of controvery over a freeway through North Oakland was ended today with city council adoption of the Grove-Shafter route agreement.

The action, on a 6-3 vote of the council yesterday, gave state highway engineers the green light for detailed planning of the $59,000,000 project, to link the Broadway tunnel with the Nimitz Freeway.

Agreement on the route already approved by the State Highway Commission came after efforts to delay action had gained an initial victory.

Advanced in opposition to the approved route was a plan presented by C. R. Armas, representing the North Oakland Home Defenders, who maintained his proposal would be cheaper, shorter, and cause less disruption of homes and business properties. . . .

Councilman Glenn E. Hoover brought order to an hour and 45 minutes of chaotic discussion.

"After all of this discussion, everyone should understand why the law specifies that freeway routes shall be determined by state officials rather than local authorities. We would rarely be able to build any freeway anywhere if we had to find a route that everybody wanted."

Oakland Tribune
July 18, 1958

Supervisors. We had hearings—one was conducted in the auditorium of Oakland Tech (where many years before I'd spoken as Student Body president). Representing both the Temescal and College Avenue merchants, I spoke in opposition to the proposal. There was a full house—the entire assembly hall was filled. We essentially said, "Stay with your existing plan—leave us alone." We got a lot of support among our friends and neighbors, but apparently it didn't reach the ears of downtown. The mayor of Oakland at the time was Clifford Rishell; he and most of the county officials went along with the state proposal, and we just couldn't raise any interest down there.

I can't say precisely why we were not successful in urging them to leave a well established neighborhood alone. I'm sure the city leaders of Berkeley resisted the original plan to have the freeway go down Ashby. And the power of the state was overwhelming. But, also, I think that Oakland and Alameda County leaders saw wealth coming because of the BART stations and the great housing and commercial developments that they thought would result.

We did succeed somewhat because they eventually redrew the plans, taking the freeway route further up around 55th Street rather than through the heart of Temescal. But we figured it a Pyrrhic victory, as they say; we won some, but we still lost a lot of homes, and many businesses were sacrificed.

I don't remember any strong resistance from any particular street or block. By law, people whose properties were demolished to make way for the freeway had to be compensated. My recollection is that people got fair compensation for their properties, which were mostly working-family homes. Some businessmen sought

Construction of Grove-Shafter Freeway and MacArthur BART Station (looking south), 1967. *Courtesy of BART*

additional compensation for finding a similar kind of building to the one they were having to vacate.

The building on the corner of 46th and Grove where my parents' had the grocery store still stands and is now a black-owned barbershop. A building that they once owned on 46th Street, midway between Grove and Shattack, was demolished for the freeway, but by then my parents had sold it. So we were not personally affected by the freeway project. But the general attitude within the neighborhood, particularly during the construction phase, was that it disrupted the community something fierce.

Change

The culture of the neighborhood changed, brought about principally by the building of the freeway but also because of the changing demographics. Some say the change was for the better, but it wasn't for many of the old-timers. By the 1960s, a lot of the Italians and Irish were moving out. There was now the influx of blacks moving into the homes and opening businesses. Aldo and I had many black clients. We had a sidewalk entrance to our office on Shattuck, as opposed to the twenty-two steps above Pete Tira's place. Clients would stroll in without appointments, and blacks became a part of our clientele. They were fine people and we melded with them.

Grove-Shafter Freeway, under construction (looking south toward downtown Oakland), June 21, 1967. *Courtesy of Department of Transportation*

42nd Street Overpass (looking east), 2005.

By 1966, I was commuting from my home in Orinda to my law practice in Temescal, going through the Caldecott Tunnel. The traffic congestion along that route and the problem of possible closure of the Caldecott in the event of an accident made it seem—I guess I convinced myself—that the freeway, and BART in particular, would solve the traffic problems of getting to and from Contra Costa and Alameda County. I reached that decision reluctantly because we lost a lot of friends and businesses that had to move out of the area.

Just as the human body heals after surgery, the neighborhood in some ways eventually became accustomed to the changes. I no longer remember as clearly the ferocity of the opposition, but it was strong then, very strong. It's human nature to resist change, of course; but the freeway had also uprooted a whole neighborhood where many people were born and raised and never left. ✦

Up until the late 1950s when the right-of-way was being bought up for the Grove-Shafter Freeway, Temescal had been relatively intact. There hadn't been any wholesale demolition or any major apartment building developments. But when the freeway went through, it wiped out a lot of great, middle-class and working-class homes. Given the fact that there hadn't been any new construction in Temescal, those people whose homes were destroyed obviously had to move elsewhere. I had a girlfriend who lived on 42nd Street, between Grove and Telegraph, whose family had to move. They'd had no more idea of moving than the man in the moon.

Ray Raineri
Temescal native and
local historian

Oakland is a major metropolitan center for the entire Bay Area and specifically for the East Bay. This means that the commercial, industrial, cultural, and other facilities of our city serve not only the citizens of Oakland but a population in excess of two million people. If the Bay Area continues to grow, as there is every indication that it will, this population may well be doubled before the end of this century. Under these circumstances, we must provide adequate transportation not simply around our city, but as close as feasible to the heart of the city as well as to its industrial and recreational areas. Thus, it is not possible to relegate freeways to purely circumferential routes. They must penetrate the city if they are to serve their function.

Corwin R. Mocine, City Planning Engineer
In a letter dated November 5, 1956, to Sewall Glinternick, publisher of the *Claremont Press*

Sewall Glinternick

Unlike many of those who took issue with the state's plan to build a freeway through Temescal and Rockridge, Sewall Glinternick was a relative newcomer to the neighborhood. He had moved to North Oakland only a few years before news of the Highway Division's proposal for the Grove-Shafter Freeway first surfaced. As editor of three local newspapers, however, he played a significant role in bringing the issue to light and keeping it before the public.

In 1954, with a master's degree in journalism from the University of Minnesota, and after four years of newspaper work in southern California, Sewall came north with his young family to become owner and publisher of a community weekly, the Claremont Press *(serving Rockridge), and two associated weeklies, the* Oakland Telegraph *(serving Temescal) and* Berkeley Telegraph *(serving Elmwood). "At one point I had around ten employees," Sewall explains, "including press operators, Linotype operators, an editor, bookkeeper, someone to handle the classified ads, and my wife, Reeva, who managed the office. It was a real culture shock to suddenly be responsible for ten other families."*

Sewall was determined to live in the area where he'd just purchased the paper and so went house hunting in both Rockridge and Temescal. After an intensive search, he and his wife found a home on Manila Avenue near 42nd Street in Temescal. "The house was old, but in move-in condition," recalls Sewall, "and it was just an absolutely delightful neighborhood. All the neighbors were old Italian families that had lived there for years, and everybody knew everybody else." These many years later, having watched all their neighbors come and go, Sewall and Reeva continue to live in their home on Manila.

Sewall sold the Claremont Press *in 1969. "I had two children and had never been on vacation with them. The demands of owning the paper meant that I had been an absentee parent, and it bothered the heck out of me." The new owners, however, soon hired him back to run the paper, and this pattern continued until the mid-1990s when he retired from newspaper work altogether. Even then, Sewall did not retire completely; a self-described workaholic, he has served since 1995 as executive director of the El Cerrito Chamber of Commerce.*

The Proposals

We heard about the proposal to build a freeway not too long after we got here. When the news came, it came like a freight train. There weren't a lot of preliminaries. I first heard about it through news releases from the Division of Highways. The law required that they hold public hearings. There was going to be a public hearing on a proposed freeway through North Oakland—actually, it was advertised as a connector freeway from the Nimitz Freeway [today's I-880] out through the tunnel to Contra Costa County. It wasn't, as I recall, "Would you like it, would you not like it?" It simply was going to be built. They were going to come in and explain this connector freeway. We naively thought that maybe they were going to ask our opinion on this, but they didn't, as we discovered. They made it very plain that money had been allocated for it, and it was going to be built! They didn't specify where exactly the freeway would go.

I'm almost certain the first meeting was held at the Columbo Club, one of the Italian social centers, on Claremont Avenue. There was a "preferred route" presented, but there were also several other routes—seven I think—presented. The map they showed us looked like a bunch of worms. It was scary. One of the alternative routes cut diagonally across Temescal's business district, but that wasn't the Division of Highway's preferred route. Their preferred route was the one they eventually built. I had the feeling all along that we were being set up. If they could get everybody upset because the freeway was coming through their area, when they finally picked a route—which I'm sure they'd picked when they started out—everybody else would heave a big sigh of relief and sit back and say, "Well, at least they didn't get us," and let them go ahead and do whatever they wanted to do.

Three North Oakland residents have filed suit in Alameda County Superior Court challenging the constitutionality of an agreement between the city and the state which cleared the way for the proposed Grove-Shafter Freeway. . . .

The agreement was signed last summer after the State Highway Commission selected the freeway route following a series of public hearings. The agreement permits the state to close and relocate approximately 33 Oakland streets when the freeway is built. . . .

The plaintiffs claim the agreement is an unconstitutional attempt to delegate the legislative powers of the city to the state.

Oakland Tribune
February 27, 1959

The North Oakland Home Defenders has lost its attempt to block the city-state agreement on the Grove-Shafter Freeway. A taxpayer's suit which had previously been turned down in superior and appellate court reached the State Supreme Court in San Francisco yesterday. By voting not to hear the matter, the high court backed the previous rulings. . . .

The association had urged an alternate route through old St. Mary's Cemetery and Richmond Blvd. They contended it would disrupt less homes and buisness properties.

Oakland Tribune
September 22, 1960

A six-lane highway would be provided from 51st St. to the Caldecott Tunnel, but enough land would be purchased to allow expansion to eight lanes. . . .

The Bay Area Rapid Transit District is anxious to run rails down the center of the Grove-Shafter, making the freeway the first such road west of Chicago.

The district has estimated that an additional 26 feet would be needed along most of the highway to make room for two sets of rails.

But 90 feet would be required where the lines serving Berkeley and Contra Costa County meet in Oakland. . . . A station is projected for that interchange.

Oakland Tribune
May 28, 1961

55th Street at Telegraph (looking west), circa 1940s. *Photo: John Harder*

I personally didn't like any of the options that were presented. One alternative had them tearing out a huge number of homes. One or two of them would have torn out two business districts, which, of course, I had to oppose, because that's how I was making my living—from advertising from those business districts. With every one of their alternatives, I could see the damage that it would cause. So, I didn't want to see the change, just for the sake of moving people from Contra Costa County to downtown Oakland.

A lot of the meetings were held at the Columbo Club. There were a couple of meetings held at Oakland Tech, that I can recall. About fifty or sixty people would come to these meetings. For a public meeting on that subject, that was a lot of people. People were upset, but most people weren't upset enough to leave their home after supper and go out to listen to a bunch of politicians.

The state and the downtown interests, namely the *Oakland Tribune,* had not been shy about trying to sell North Oakland on the idea that it would get a lot of traffic off the streets. But they tried to sell it to people who didn't particularly want to see the character of their neighborhood change. The resistance to change is universal, and the resistance in Temescal and Rockridge was no more or less. The people there looked at their neighborhood and said, "We've got a pretty good neighborhood. We like it here. We

City Manager Wayne E. Thompson today asked the Oakland City Council to reaffirm its request for a "co-ordinated and mutually satisfactory solution" of the controversy over plans to combine rapid transit with the Grove-Shafter Freeway at the earliest possible date.

Thompson reminded that the immediate problem concerns the construction of a portion of the freeway from MacArthur Blvd. to 42nd St. for which funds are available and plans virtually complete.

Highway officials, with backing from the the Oakland Chamber of Commerce, are insisting on an immediate start on this section without transit.

Oakland Tribune
April 18, 1963

The Chabot Canyon Association is locked in a battle with the state over dirt, noise and the relocation of a proposed rapid transit line.

The association, a group of homeowners in a plush north Oakland residential area, is seeking to prevent the State Division of Highways from building a 12-lane freeway through the heart of this canyon community. . . .

Recently, the group won the first round in what promises to be a long, long battle. . . . [R]epresentatives appearing before the State Division of Highways got the state group to halt plans on the proposed Grove-Shafter Freeway.

San Francisco Examiner
March 2, 1964

Bids will be opened June 22 for one of the largest freeway construction contracts in California history—the 60-mile-an-hour interchange of the Grove-Shafter and MacArthur Freeways. . . . The eight-lane freeway project will extend from 24th to 53rd Streets as the first unit of the Grove-Shafter Freeway. . . .

The shell for BART's MacArthur station will be constructed just north of the intersection with the MacArthur Freeway, and transit tracks will be placed in the median of the Grove-Shafter Freeway.

The Alameda County Flood Control and Water Conservation District is contributing $44,000 for a drainage culvert for Temescal Creek.

Oakland Tribune
June 3, 1966

don't want to see it change." This wasn't the young people, of course, because they'd already started to gravitate toward what appeared to be the greener grass on the other side of the Caldecott Tunnel.

Give People Compensation

I haven't had much dealings with Caltrans, which is the child of the Division of Highways, but back then the Division of Highways had things locked up. Once it became obvious that we really weren't being consulted about the freeway route, I suggested that they at least pay tenants for relocation costs. They told me to go take a hike. I kept pointing out, "Owners of property were being compensated for their land, surely you can compensate people for the cost of moving." It seemed so logical to me that I could not understand why they just dismissed it out of hand. Why they dismissed it out of hand, is because they didn't feel they had to do anything they didn't want to do.

More than 15 alignments, or combination of alignments, were given careful study by the Division of Highways, and several other routings suggested by private citizens, both at the engineering hearings and at the Commission hearing, were given preliminary studies which were carried to the point of indicating such other alignments were impractical.

Highway Commission Report, 1958

I wish I could say it was altruism that got me involved in this issue, but it was anger. I was a tenant. I had the print shop behind a house on the east side of Telegraph at 56th Street, which they were going to take for one of the freeway offramps. I wanted moving expenses. It costs money to move. When you have a business like a print shop, you don't just hire Starving Students to come with their truck and haul your equipment away. You need experts—people who know how to move presses, Linotype machines. This is all stuff that is delicately balanced. You mess it up and it isn't going to work. So, that became my main focus.

A lot of people in the legislature whom I approached—and I'd talk to anybody who would talk to me—thought it was a logical extension of what the Division of Highways was doing with the property owners. It didn't strike them as ridiculous that you would pay an owner to take his property, and moving costs to the person who was living on that property or had a business at that property on a lease basis. When they had long term leases, these people would buy out the lease, of course, because they had

Grove-Shafter Freeway, under construction (looking north toward Berkeley), April 11, 1968. *Courtesy of Department of Transportation*

Grove-Shafter Freeway, under construction (looking east toward the Caldecott Tunnel), October 10, 1968. *Courtesy of Department of Transportation*

to. But they didn't feel they had to pay anybody to move anywhere. "That's not our worry, buddy," they said. Well, it was a worry for all these people who were being forced to move. And a lot of those people were not well to do, who could afford it.

Randolph Collier, known as the "Father of the American Freeways." *Courtesy of California State Archives*

The senate legislative committee that handled this was headed by a guy named Randolph Collier. Senator Collier was a well known spokesman for the Division of Highways. Whatever the Division of Highways wanted, Collier gave it to them. I tried approaching him a couple of times, and he just gave me short shrift. He wasn't going to listen to anything that the Division of Highways hadn't approved—and he told me so. So, in my effort to get moving costs for tenants, I worked around him. Instead, I depended on the Democratic Party organization that existed at the time to get my point across in the legislature.

I was stubborn enough and had enough knowledge of politics to understand that there were some allies in Sacramento that I could make good use of. Local representatives—even local county supervisors—helped. But, Jesse Unruh, who was speaker of the State Assembly, was feuding with the governor at the time. You wouldn't believe the political efforts it took to get both of them to agree to let the bill that allocated funds for these things go through, when no other funding bill was going through.

There was a lot of tugging and hollering, but we eventually got what we wanted from the legislature, and the governor signed the bill. But then the Division of Highways gave their interpretation of what the legislature had done, and they turned the will of the legislature on its head. They decided that the bill indicated that they *didn't* have to pay compensation to tenants for moving expenses. I went to the legislative advocate and asked, "What does the bill say?" He gave his written opinion of what the bill said. I said, "OK, I agree with your opinion. Now tell the Division of Highways that that's your view." He asked why, and I showed him the Division of Highways' interpretation, and he said that was absolutely ludicrous. And so he told them, "Hey, shape up. Your interpretation is dead wrong, and you'd have to be a little bit foolish to believe it." And so finally, in their benevolence, they sent out a press release saying that regardless of the interpretation which their attorneys have of this, they are going to give people compensation to move.

The selection of the total alignment including the C-3 (Revised) section was supported by the Oakland Chamber of Commerce, the Alameda County Highway Advisory Committee, and the City Engineer and technical staff of the City of Oakland.

Highway Commission Report, 1958

In Oakland, planners and boosters after World War II promoted a regional, metropolitan distribution of industrial investment and growth, campaigning nationally for factories, warehouses, and other facilties for the city's urban periphery. This initially benefited but ironically ultimately undermined Oakland itself.

Robert O. Self
from *American Babylon*

52nd Street at Grove (looking east), during construction of the Grove-Shafter Freeway and BART, circa 1968. *Courtesy of the Oakland Cultural Heritage Survey*

In Temescal, a lot of good housing stock was leveled. The customer base, of course, was reduced. There weren't the same number of people shopping at the Fairway Market [Vern's] or at the other businesses up and down Telegraph Avenue. It removed a sizable slice of humanity that the area had depended upon for its economic lifeblood.

Ray Raineri
Temescal native and local historian

52nd Street at Martin Luther King Jr. Way (looking east), 2005.

The meetings and hearings held by the Division of Highways prior to the time that the State Highway Engineer made his recommendation February 13, 1958, had resulted in a substantial agreement as to the proper location of a major portion of the section of state highways under consideration.

Highway Commission Report, 1958

The Chosen Route

All this happened a few years after the preferred route had been announced—the preferred route being the present route of the Grove-Shafter Freeway. When they officially declared the chosen route, there was a good deal of rumbling among those affected by the decision. But their strategy of discouraging protest by laying out six or seven alternatives, and then relieving the people along those routes of worry because theirs hadn't been picked, worked. They all figured they were home free. They weren't looking at it in the long term; they weren't looking at what it would do to their neighborhood as a whole. They only looked at how it affected their own home. I don't fault people for that. Like I say, I got mad about the compensation for tenants because I was a tenant who wasn't being compensated. There was darn little altruism in it. There was anger for other people in the same boat—I thought we were all getting had—but my first concern was the fact that *I* was getting had.

Freeway and Rockridge BART station, under construction, January 1968. *Courtesy of BART*

We moved our newspaper office into a storefront on Hudson, near Claremont, (where the Dance Space studio is now). This was after the lower section of the Grove-Shafter—from below the 580 interchange to Claremont Avenue—had opened in 1969, and they were about to start construction on the part through Rockridge.

When the lower part opened, they held this luncheon to extol the new freeway's beauties. At the luncheon, Manny Razeto, who was a county supervisor, got up and

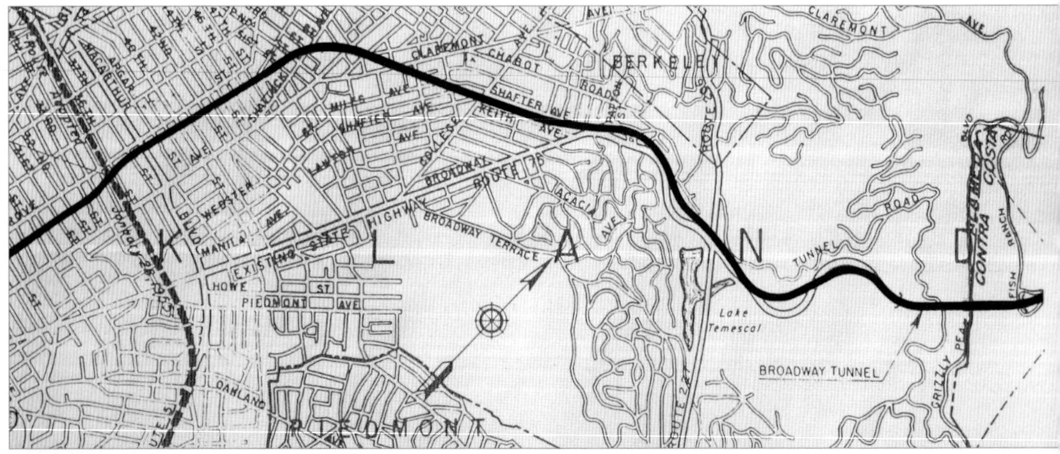

Division of Highways map (detail) showing a portion of the adopted Grove-Shafter Freeway route, 1958. *Courtesy of Department of Transportation*

said that the freeway should be named after a good Italian, because, after all, it sliced right through the Temescal neighborhood. Then I got up and said to him and everyone else that he was right—it would be *most* appropriate to name it after the mobster, Al Capone! The representative of the Division of Highways didn't think that was very funny.

I said this because their version of the democratic process was, "We'll tell you what to do and you'd better damn well do it." I never had the feeling that the Division of Highways really gave a damn about pleasing the people of North Oakland. They never created that impression; they never *worked* to create that impression.

Oakland City Councilman Joshua Rose (left), Donna Lencioni, and Alameda County Supervisor Emanuel Razeto, at ribbon cutting ceremony marking the opening of the first phase of the Grove-Shafter Freeway, July 23, 1969. *Courtesy of the Oakland History Room*

They approached a problem that was real. They knew that if they told people what they had to do, people would not like it. So they gave people all sorts of "choices." Except that they didn't really. When it was all through, after all these public hearings, lo and behold, the first route they suggested was the route *they* picked.

Two Neighborhoods

The chosen route did probably minimize the amount of damage to the business districts, at least on Telegraph. College Avenue was affected more. They went past the business district on Telegraph somewhat; but they cut through the heart of the business district on College, and took out a number of businesses, many of whom were my advertisers. So I had a vested interest in keeping the districts as intact as possible.

But, the freeway split North Oakland in half. Temescal, Rockridge, North Oakland, had been more or less one large community. Italians and Portuguese lived in all of the different sections—not just in Temescal. It made two neighborhoods instead of one. It used to be North Oakland; now it's two separate entities. In effect it probably hurt a lot of businesses.

College Avenue, at Shafter (buildings demolished), 1949. *Courtesy of the Oakland History Room*

The commercial district on College, before the freeway, was self-contained. You didn't have to go to Berkeley or downtown Oakland or anyplace else to meet your day-to-day needs. The freeway, I think, altered the buying habits of people and as a result altered the nature of the businesses in both Rockridge and Temescal. A lot of the food markets on College Avenue disappeared. The hardware store disappeared, and in their place came a plethora of antique shops.

Temescal took longer to change. As a district, it was totally different from Rockridge. In Rockridge there had been a lot of ebb and flow—people moving in, people moving out. Temescal for a very long time had been a very stable community. There were still a lot of the older Italians living there, people who had come to this country, purchased their own homes for the first time. Once they bought them, they weren't about to move away to the suburbs. But their children did, just as quick as they could. Their kids were educated and upwardly mobile. Temescal didn't fit their station. Temescal was an old Italian neighborhood, and the younger generation weren't old Italians.

Those kids growing up and moving to Orinda, Moraga, or Lafayette, and the older people dying off—that's what started the change in Temescal. People started selling off their homes, and they'd sell them to anybody who'd buy. Negroes who had been confined to areas like in West Oakland suddenly could buy in Temescal. I think this would have happened whether the freeway went in or not. I just think the freeway hastened it.

The building of the Grove Shafter Freeway was sad, because it took so long. The aquisition and then the property just seemed to lie idle there, fenced. It was years before they got to working on it.

And it was a sweep right through the middle. We had quite a little business district around 55th and Telegraph. There was Idora Realty, Nolan's Bar, the Persian rug business (that moved up to College), a meat market, Cunio's little grocery. On 55th Street, there had been a row of homes—all the way to Shattuck.

Aldo Guidotti

There used to be a business district along Claremont Avenue, and the freeway, which goes through at an angle, just destroyed it. The freeway also created a barrier separating the Temescal neighborhood from the neighborhood west of the freeway, which became kind of a no-man's land. It's isolated, and there's really no commercial district there now.

Donald Hausler

Sofa on sidewalk, 42nd Street overpass, 2005.

(Assemblyman Ken) Meade feels all freeway proposals must be reviewed in light of current needs and desires of the people. Also that rapid transit must be given the chance to function before new freeways are built which disrupt the environment and are costly to the taxpayers.

. . . Oakland city council's recently adopted comprehensive policy plan . . . states that the council will oppose all new freeway construction in Oakland which would increase problems without compensating benefits. Any construction must serve the transportation needs of Oakland's residents, not just those of commuters, under the new policy.

The city policy statements say any future freeway construction must not "destroy or disrupt" neighborhoods or impose unnecessary barriers between them. . . .

The policy says the council is attempting "to prevent Oakland from being sacrificed for the commuting convenience of suburban dwellers."

Montclarion, November 17, 1971

A Rosy Prediction

If the freeway had any value to North Oakland, it's that for a while it got a lot of traffic off the streets by eliminating a great deal of through traffic from people who lived beyond the tunnel but worked in downtown Oakland or San Francisco. In retrospect, however, building freeways, or expanding them, makes no sense. If you look at all of the projections for the freeways here in the Bay Area, they all say the same thing: in five years from now, wherever you're going, it will take you a half-hour longer to get there. I suspect that's probably a rosy prediction.

The problems that the freeways have to solve are also social problems, economic problems—problems that have nothing at all to do with transportation. What appears to be a nifty solution turns out to be a horror story. We try to keep pace by increasing the number of freeways, or the number of lanes, but we can't do it.

One of the problems we face is we're not creating the jobs where we're building houses. We're forcing people to get in their car to go to work. As long as we keep separating people from their jobs, we're going to need more and more roads as more and more people move further out to where there are more affordable homes. The more they build cheap housing further out, and the roads for people to get there, the more people will be commuting. It's that pattern that makes new freeways obsolete before they're even opened. ✦

Freeway sign, 42nd Street overpass, 2005.

Business district at Telegraph and 55th Street (looking north), circa 1945. *John Harder Collection*

Highway 24 overpass, Telegraph and 55th Street (looking north), 2005.

The first section of the Grove-Shafter Freeway through north Oakland was opened yesterday with appropriate ceremonies—and the blessing of the Italian-Americans who live along its route.

Alameda County Supervisor Emanuel P. Razeto, who represents north Oakland and is a native of Genoa, Italy, suggested during a lunch, following 11 a.m. ribbon-cutting ceremonies, that the freeway be named for some distinguished "Italian-American." . . .

The freeway, he said, "trespassed" on the area and to many was considered "a disaster" until combined with Bay Area Rapid Transit tracks, which will use the highway median. . . .

"The Grove-Shafter cuts through an Italian community," Razeto said. "America was named after an Italian."

Oakland City Councilman J. R. Rose, a Negro, good-naturedly told Razeto the freeway "also passes through a good black neighborhood."

Oakland Tribune
July 24, 1969

East Bay Negro Historical Society

The Rise of an Organization at Temescal's Shifting Edge

Introduction

With the closure of the war industries and government-approved housing in the East Bay following World War II, thousands of African Americans in West Oakland suddenly found themselves in search of a new home. Many crossed over the long-standing racial divide around 36th Street and into the area of North Oakland that historically had been considered part of greater Temescal. Throughout the 1950s, this area—from Grove Street west to the Emeryville border, and from West MacArthur north toward Berkeley—became increasingly integrated as African Americans replaced older residents largely of Italian, Irish, or Portuguese descent.

Grove and 38th Street (looking west), 1935. *Courtesy of the Oakland History Room*

Meanwhile, Grove Street continued to persist as the racial divide east of which African Americans generally were not welcome. In the 1960s, as the demolition of homes for the Grove-Shafter Freeway right-of-way and the resulting drop in property values knocked the wind out of the Grove Street business district, it appeared as if the freeway would reinforce Grove Street as a racial "redline." At this now economically blighted edge—no longer defined by discriminatory lending and real estate practices but by the new freeway—the modest but visionary East Bay Negro Historical Society planted itself.

The humble birth of the Society in 1965, and its gradual maturation into what is today the acclaimed African American Museum and Library at Oakland (AAMLO) on 14th Street and Martin Luther King Jr. Way, is a story that is as remarkable as it is largely unknown. This alone makes it worth telling. What makes it also a Temescal story is that from its founding in 1965 until 1982 when the Society moved to the Golden Gate Branch Library on San Pablo Avenue, the organization's headquarters were in three successive locations, all on or near Grove Street—what Ray Mellana described as once having been the western boundary of "the real core of Temescal."

Through interviews with Madison Harvey, Gladys Jordan, and Donald Hausler, we learn how vision, tenacity, skill, timing, and outside support eventually led to a secure future for the organization and its final

Greyhound bus terminal, Memphis, Tennessee, 1943. *Photo: Esther Bubley; courtesy of the Library of Congress*

move in 2002 to its permanent home near downtown Oakland. Reading their stories, we also see how discrimination in employment, housing, education, and public services that persisted in Oakland before and after World War II contributed to the cultural milieu out of which the East Bay Negro Historical Society emerged.

Interwoven with this, Ray Raineri's recollections of growing up in the neighborhood immediately to the west of Grove, "out of Temescal by a block or two," provide a personal look at how shifting demographics and *de facto* segregation manifested in Temescal and adjacent North Oakland neighborhoods. Ray's accounts, together with excerpts from other sources, serve as a backdrop to the East Bay Negro Historical Society's story while amplifying some of the underlying social forces that have contributed to changes in Temescal's boundaries, makeup, and identity.

Just when the route of the Grove-Shafter Freeway seemed poised to reinforce Grove Street as a racial divide, California's landmark Fair Housing Act of 1963, pushed through by African American state assemblymember from Berkeley, William Byron Rumford, helped make it possible for African Americans in search of housing and business locations to cross Grove to the eastern side of the freeway and into Temescal. (One wonders whether officials were aware of this paradox when, in 1980, they renamed a section of the Grove-Shafter the William Byron Rumford Freeway.) Lower commercial rents along Shattuck and Telegraph, and a somewhat depressed housing market in Temescal—partially a consequence of the new freeway—also contributed by keeping the traditionally working-class Temescal affordable.

BART and freeway under construction, Grove, near 47th Street (looking north), circa 1967. *Courtesy of the Oakland Cultural Heritage Survey*

As Sewall Glinternick described in the previous chapter, throughout the 1970s and 1980s, African Americans stepped up their migration into Temescal as older, largely Italian American homeowners died or moved away. Over the past decade, however, this trend has reversed. Korean, Ethiopian, and Eritrean businesses and families now contribute to Temescal's diversity, but with the turnover of the neighborhood's older generation of African Americans, fewer younger African American families are moving into Temescal. Once again, the neighborhood's demographics are dramatically shifting as Temescal's soaring real estate market defines who can and cannot afford to live here. In the process, just as the East Bay Negro Historical Society eventually moved away from Temescal, will African Americans in the neighborhood again be a rarity?

A realtor should never be instrumental in introducing into a neighborhood . . . members of any race or nationality or any individuals whose presence will be clearly detrimental to property values in that neighborhood.

Code of Ethics, National Association of Real Estate Boards, 1924

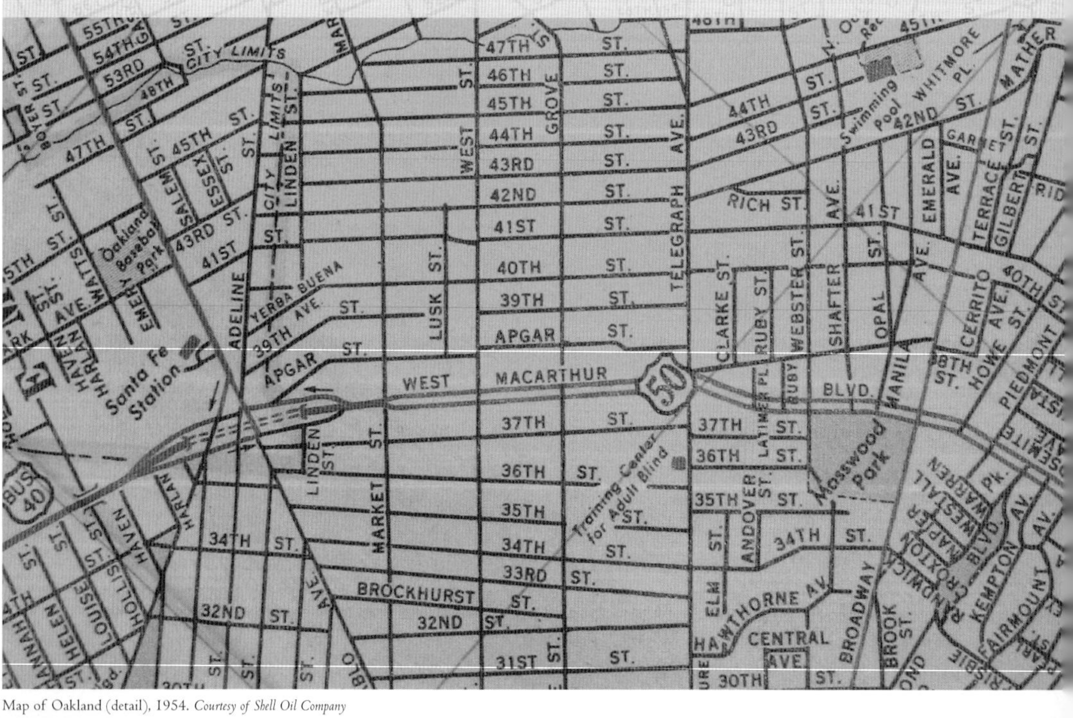

Map of Oakland (detail), 1954. *Courtesy of Shell Oil Company*

Madison Harvey

Of those who met on Sunday, July 2, 1965, at the Apgar Street home of Dr. Marcella and Jesse Ford to formally establish the East Bay Negro Historical Society, Madison Harvey was the youngest. Whereas Morrie Turner was a mere five years his senior, all the other original founders—the Fords, Eugene and Ruth Lasartemay, and E. Harold Mason—were at least a generation older. So, although Madison had been one of the key promoters of African American history and culture in the East Bay, including having served as secretary of the Carter G. Woodson Historical Society upon its founding in 1956 and as a columnist for black-owned newspapers such as the California Voice *and* Oakland Post, *he still felt a bit like the youngster. "Whatever the older people wanted me to do," he recalls, "they'd tell me, and I'd do it. That's how things were done."*

Over the years since then, Madison has seen the East Bay Negro Historical Society grow from a grassroots group without a permanent home into a modern archive and museum at the beautifully restored former Charles Greene Library on 14th Street, at the edge of downtown Oakland. For Madison, the organization's huge leap in professionalism and its move away from the kinds of volunteer, hands-on activities that he once enjoyed, combined with a recent disability, have sidelined him from active participation in AAMLO. Nevertheless, at 76, Madison remains passionate about the full range of African American cultural expression. "Unfortunately," he admits wistfully, "it's still too often the case that black people just simply are not interested in knowing about their own past."

Since moving in 2000 from his home in West Oakland to a residential facility for seniors on San Pablo and 32nd Street, Madison has continued to research, write, and on occasion mount exhibits about black heritage. In doing so, he carries on the tradition of the older founders who, fifty years ago, were devoting their lives to understanding and sharing the diverse contributions that African Americans have made to the East Bay, California, America, and beyond.

Settling in Oakland

I was born in a little community called Colbert, Oklahoma, in 1928. Colbert is in Bryan County, on the Red River, which forms part of the border with Texas. I was born and raised on the farm that my dad owned.

I joined the Navy at the end of high school, in 1947. I was sent to San Diego for boot training, and then to Oakland. When I got out of the Navy in the early 1950s, I stayed here.

A lot of my relatives settled here, too. Numerous cousins—the same generation of family from back home—all sort of drifted this way. I had a brother here, and not long after I left the Navy, I persuaded my mother and father to join us.

When I arrived in 1947, the majority of black folk lived in West Oakland. There was a very sharp dividing line between West Oakland and the rest of the community. South Berkeley had a thickly settled community along Sacramento Street, consisting of some of the leading black personalities in the area. Oakland's black community was centered in the area from 7th Street and Peralta, up to what is now the 580 Freeway. There were very few blacks north of what is now West MacArthur. But blacks were beginning to scatter. They were moving beyond that line and filling up areas of North Oakland, towards Berkeley. In the 1950s, my parents and I bought a house on 57th Street, just off of Market Street. At the time, it was mostly white, large, Catholic families who lived there.

I became active in church—the South Berkeley Community Church, which is at Fairview and Ellis Street, just off of Grove—what is now Martin Luther King Jr. Way. South Berkeley Community Church was on an adventure of its own—it was integrated. That was significant in those days, because when the church was organized in 1944, you just didn't have integrated churches. I've belonged to that church for over fifty years.

After I left the Navy, I worked my first summer in Oakland at the Naval Air Station. After that, I went to school, first at the University of California, and then at West Contra Costa Junior College. As I was finishing up there, I became part of a

Beginning even before the [1906] earthquake, the market for Oakland and Berkeley housing soared as real estate and streetcar line developers worked hand in hand to open and promote new housing tracts. These new neighborhoods were planned in accord with the then-new ideology of the "city beautiful," which stressed harmony with the environment and protection from unpleasant intrusions. . . . The new tracts were governed by homeowners' agreements which . . . required pledges to maintain homes and yards. They also forbade the sale of properties to blacks or Asians.

Visions Toward Tomorrow: The History of the East Bay Afro-American Community, 1852-1977

The Selective Service Act was passed on May 18, 1917, which allowed blacks to be drafted. When a group of African-American draftees left Oakland for basic training the mayor of Oakland and a city councilman addressed the men and wished them luck in their effort to keep democracy alive abroad. Two days later, as the troops left, the Oakland City Council considered a restrictive housing ordinance for the Santa Fe Tract, a white neighborhood. Both the mayor and councilman who addressed the departing black troops favored the restrictive covenant.

Parallel Communities: African Americans in California's East Bay

In our neighborhood, next to the Italians, there were probably a lot of Irish. The only black families that I knew of were a husband and wife who lived on 42nd Street, between West and Lusk–he worked for the Oakland Fire Department–and a gentleman named Mr. Johnson whom my mother and father spoke of very favorably when I was very young. Evidently, he lived near Lusk and 42nd Street. According to my mother, he had organized what was called the North Oakland Improvement Association. He was interested in the beautification of the area, in particular the planting of flowers and trees. There was also a black family–the Logwoods–on 41st Street, between Lusk and Market. According to my parents, they had been there for many, many years. That was about it for the first six, eight years of my life, into the early 1940s.

My earliest recollection of a black-owned business was a cleaners directly across the street from Longfellow Elementary School on Apgar and Market. This was as early as the mid- to late-1940s. By 1950, a medical doctor, LeGrand Lawson Coleman, had built an office on 41st and Market. Around that time, Kermit Wilson, brother of former mayor Lionel Wilson, opened a dentistry practice across from Longfellow. Otherwise, black-owned businesses were very, very scarce.

Ray Raineri, who grew up on 42nd and Market Street

group—what I would now call a "minority team"—that was hired by Chevron Research. I was the first Negro hired by them, which was then a division of Standard Oil. There was someone who was Chinese, another was Mexican. There were five or six of us. I worked there as a lab assistant for fourteen years. In 1969, I resigned. My parents by then had died, and I just wanted to do something else.

In 1970, I went to work for Golden State Mutual Life Insurance Company, which was an old, Negro insurance company that at the time was the third or fourth biggest black-owned business in America. I stayed there fourteen years, as well, until I left in 1984. After that, all my time went into various historical clubs and community activities.

Black Pride, Black History

Back in the 9th and 10th grades, I lived with an uncle in Ottawa, Kansas, which was right above Tulsa. There was segregation, but the schools were integrated. Ottawa was a small, western town, but there were a lot of prosperous farmers, and the school had a very high rating. There were few blacks in Kansas where I spent those two years.

I finished high school in Tulsa. In Oklahoma, of course, everything was segregated, but Tulsa had some top quality schools—white *and* black. Most of the teachers that I came up under in Tulsa were black people. They were all top-quality, Southern-educated Negroes. The little farming communities were poor, but they had high standards! We were taught Negro history there—one of the teachers at

Booker T. Washington High, in Tulsa, wrote the textbook that we used. We had school activities that taught us our history and how to be proud. It was always a question of racial pride, though we didn't use that term back then.

After I came to Oakland in 1947, I became involved in the same thing. There must have been a dozen clubs and study groups of one kind or another, including the Carter G. Woodson Historical Society, which was formed in 1956. We would have meetings every week or every month where we'd discuss Negro history. E. Harold Mason was very instrumental in the black history organizations and study groups here at the time. He traveled a great deal, lecturing, and was in touch with professors all across the country—Southern professors especially. He was a virtual encyclopedia of Negro history.

E. Harold Mason. *Courtesy of the Oakland History Room*

Marcella Ford had been a teacher at Shaw University, back in North Carolina, and she was always promoting black history education here. In the early 1960s, she organized the first class in black history at the Berkeley Adult School. Her husband, Jesse Ford, had left Tulsa when the race riots started there in 1921. That was years before my time in Tulsa, but it brought us together, once we met out here. Mr. Ford was an amateur writer and collector. He collected obituaries: if you died, he had your obit!

Marcella Ford, at the Berkeley Adult School, circa 1962. *Courtesy of the Oakland History Room*

Ruth and Eugene Lasartemay were collectors, too. People were constantly donating newspaper clippings and stuff to them—just boxes of it, which they would keep in their house on Hearst Street in Berkeley. Back in the 1940s or so, Mr. Lasartemay dug out his basement to create a storage area and a meeting room. He got down there and dug it out himself! The Lasartemays organized literally dozens of cultural clubs. The Fords and the Lasartemays had been very active

I went to Longfellow Elementary School on 39th and Market. My parents had gone there, my aunt, cousin, and brother had gone there. I graduated in June of 1950. When I started at Longfellow in 1944, the school was racially mixed, and there was one black teacher. By the time I graduated, there were very few Caucasian students–it was predominantly black. A lot of my time, up to the sixth grade, was spent with kids that attended Longfellow with me. Almost without exception, they were black kids, whose families had come into Oakland at some point after the beginning of World War II, and who lived, by and large, on the south side of MacArthur. MacArthur was almost a barrier, if you will, to minorities wanting to move into North Oakland.

Ray Raineri

in Beth Eden Baptist Church in West Oakland, one of the leading black churches here. So, whatever they were involved in, the whole community was involved in.

I had been active all along in the weekly meeting groups. We'd subscribe to journals; we'd have speakers from Africa, mostly through the efforts of Mr. Mason. Mrs. Ford was interested in the educational part. We'd have displays of Negro history, and material would come from all over. The Lasartemays went around speaking to black groups and schools. As for my role, whatever the older people wanted, they just said it. If they didn't, it wouldn't get done.

One Sunday Afternoon

Between them—Mr. Mason, the Lasartemays, and the Fords—they conceived the idea of organizing the East Bay Negro Historical Society. They had been talking about it for years. I was invited to Mrs. Ford's house one Sunday afternoon in 1965 for the initial meeting. They were all there, except for Mr. Mason, who had to be away that day. Morrie Turner, who is the well known creator of the Wee Pals comic strip, was also there. He was working for the Oakland Police Department then, but he was also a cartoonist for various black community newspapers.

Some years earlier, the Lasartemays had left Beth Eden because of a split in the church. They helped form another church, the Church of the Good Shepherd, on 52nd Street just off Grove, across from Children's Hospital. When the Historical Society came together in 1965, that's where we held our meetings. Our first repository was something that Mr. Lasartemay had rigged up—it was like a sewing box—which we carried back and forth to our meetings at the church. That was the Historical Society's first archives! We had something

Church of the Good Shepherd, 52nd Street and West, 2005.

In addition to their role as the heart of the black community, black churches nurtured the men and women who became the organizers and leaders of secular institutions which contributed in direct and practical ways to solving community problems. . . . The North Oakland Improvement Association, founded on August 4, 1925 . . . invited city officials to make presentations at its meetings and successfully lobbied for services; among the accomplishments of its first months were the promise of a traffic policeman to protect children coming and going around Longfellow School and the placement of city trash containers at various sites along Market Street to improve the general appearance and cleanliness of the area.

Visions Toward Tomorrow

East Bay Negro Historical Society storefront, 3651 Grove, 1972. *Courtesy of AAMLO*

3651 Martin Luther King Jr. Way, 2005.

going all the time. We'd sponsor shows and demonstrations, either as the Historical Society or as part of one of the other groups. It was all the same people.

The secretary of the Historical Society was Yvonne Cam. For years she'd been the secretary of our study groups, before we formalized. If there was a study group, she was part of it. She was a librarian at the West Oakland Branch, which was then on Peralta just off of Seventh Street. Her parents lived at 4614 Grove. Her father's property was that first house—with the little storefront—right where the entrance ramp now curves around and goes up onto the freeway. The building is still there. They were from Louisiana. They were light-skinned people, but they were just like a white family—there was a large population of light-skinned Negroes in those days. Yvonne was always a part of black groups, and she was always a prime mover in promoting black history in the West Oakland community. She was also a very active member of Sacred Heart Catholic Church on 40th Street.

Former Cam residence, 4614 Martin Luther King Jr. Way, 2005.

Mayors John H. Reading of Oakland and Wallace Johnson of Berkeley have proclaimed today through next Sunday as National Negro History Week.

Exhibits on the theme "African Civilization and Culture—A Worthy Historical Background," will be displayed at the East Bay Negro Historical Society, Inc., 3651 Grove St., on Mondays, Wednesdays and Fridays from noon to 5 p.m. all this month.

Oakland Tribune
February 7, 1971

Meanwhile, we kept getting material, but we'd run out of places to put it. In 1970, the Lasartemays were able to get use of a storefront on the corner of Grove and 37th Street. The Oakland Museum donated display cases. Mr. and Mrs. Lasartemay ran the place, put up the exhibits, kept the records. As far as I know, they got no pay for devoting their time to operating the organization. Personally, I think Mrs. Lasartemay's health failed because of all the years she was inhaling those musty old newspapers. The building was old, too, and there were leaks all over the place. In 1976, the Society moved to another storefront on Grove, just above 45th Street.

Second storefront location of the East Bay Negro Historical Society, 4519 Grove, 1982. *Courtesy of the African American Museum and Library at Oakland (AAMLO)*

As for the boundaries of Temescal, this is where you get a number of different interpretations, depending on who you ask. Towards the northern end, I'd have to include Idora Park—the houses that were built on the footprint of the amusement park that had extended above 56th Street for a few blocks. The northern boundary would be 58th Street, extending west to Shattuck, and in the other direction, maybe to Claremont. Arguably you'd have to go with 40th Street as Temescal's southern boundary. Going toward the hills, it would be College and Broadway. On the west end, probably Grove Street would be realistic. My family, on 42nd and Market, was out of Temescal by a block or two. We referred to where we lived as North Oakland.

Ray Raineri

The Outskirts of Town

Before the freeway and BART, Grove Street had been a very dense commercial district—especially around 55th Street, but all the way down to Berkeley. Where the Society had its storefront at 45th and Grove, there had been more of this same kind of thing. The freeway changed things considerably. It made a dividing line all through Oakland and into Berkeley. It took out a huge section of black Oakland. It pretty well wiped out Grove Street, where there had been a lot of well-established businesses.

Grove at 43rd Street (looking north), circa 1967. *Courtesy of the Oakland Cultural Heritage Survey*

I was not really aware of Temescal as a neighborhood. You might say that it was on the outskirts of town. I knew there was the Temescal library up there—because I'd roamed around all the libraries. And I think I knew that there was a Temescal swimming pool. But Temescal, as a neighborhood, just did not register with me.

In 1970, Golden State Insurance opened up at 4844 Telegraph. Before that, they'd had an office in downtown Oakland and small places in some other locations. Golden State's move was part of the pattern of black businesses moving out of the older black areas and into white areas. Somehow or other we always thought we had it made if we moved into a white area.

That same year, I started working for Golden State. The agency room was at the Telegraph office, so of course I went there. It was only then that I became aware that there was a Temescal. I had several customers on the other side of Telegraph further north. At 61st, 62nd Street, that whole neighborhood had changed to black. Before that, I didn't know anybody up there.

I think it was in the 1960s that black people began to move into the Idora Park area. Idora used to be lily-white. Back then I'd drive through there just to look at the beautiful Christmas decorations. If blacks lived there, they were light-skinned blacks, so nobody knew. I had a relative who worked downtown at Sears during the lily-white years. Nobody knew he wasn't white. I don't call that integration. It's *not* integration. In that sense, I think we can say that there had been no blacks in Idora. But then black people with money started buying there. Black people with *security*! When they started moving in, they just moved in droves. Somebody broke the line.

Carberry Street, Idora Park, 2005.

What would happen is that a real estate person—often a black realtor—would push like hell to buy a home in what was essentially a homogeneous, white, middle class neighborhood. They'd find a guy who wanted to move badly. A realtor would go in and offer him a ton of money for his house. He couldn't say no, because he'd just been offered way more than it's worth. Then the realtor would find a black family to sell that home to. Now there's one home on the block where there's a black family living. Five or six of the other families on the block would panic and say, "Oh, God, the neighborhood is changing. We'd better get out while we can." So, all of a sudden, three or four homes on that block would go up for sale. Now these people would want nothing but out, and so a gentleman comes along and says, "You want nothing but out? I'll get you somebody to buy your home." He'd go out and find a black individual who wants to buy a home in this neighborhood and who has the money to do it. And for every home that was sold, more people were going to panic. That initial effort to integrate a neighborhood was called blockbusting.

This happened in the Idora Park neighborhood, which was predominantly Italian. I remember this because I knew the realtor who was primarily responsible for it. If he couldn't get the Italian families to move in, then upwardly mobile black families were just as good. The realtor was not African American, he was just a sharp businessman.

Sewall Glinternick

A Different Style

The Historical Society continued to grow. In the early 1980s we moved from 45th and Grove to the Golden Gate Branch Library on San Pablo. And other people came in—professionals. Lawrence Crouchett, as I recall, was the organization's first professional director—and real scholar. He brought a different style of doing things. Robert Haynes later came in as a curator. In the storefronts on Grove, the Lasartemays had every scrap of paper that ever was published on the walls! You could walk in there and you'd *never* finish reading all the stuff. That was in the old days, when all you had were clippings. You'd cut them out, put them on pieces of pasteboard, and put them on the wall. Dr. Crouchett changed all that. The exhibits were more professional, more polished, and they focused on specific themes. And he knew how to get grants. The Society changed its name to the African American Museum and Library at Oakland—AAMLO. Its move into the renovated library building down on 14th Street was chiefly his doing.

Having a director can open up a lot of things for you, and it can block a lot of things. As the organization evolved, it developed professional standards; but at the same time, it shut out the older, grassroots kind of people. You'd go in and look around, but there was nothing for you to do. Somebody else had already done everything. It's not easy being a director of an organization. It's not easy making everybody happy.

Over the last few years, I've managed to keep putting out some historical publications. In the activities room downstairs where I live, I've put together an exhibit. But before moving here in 2000, I had to throw away boxes and boxes of clippings—I was so disappointed. I don't go to AAMLO anymore, not since I became disabled. I used to go there all the time, but I sold my car a year ago, and that cut out my circulation. And they have a system now where you need an appointment. At the Oakland History Room at the main library, everything is open. For someone like me, who likes to browse, it makes a big difference. I'll be glad when I can start going again. ✦

Front cover of *The Whip-O-Will*, Vol. I, No. I, July 2003, published by Madison Harvey. *Courtesy of Madison Harvey*

Gladys Meriewether Jordan

While Gladys Jordan was not among those who met at the Ford's on that auspicious Sunday in 1965 when the East Bay Negro Historical Society was formally organized, she had crossed paths often with the Fords and the Lasartemays in their shared quest for material on African American history. As a teacher at Tompkins Elementary School in West Oakland beginning in 1948, and later at Santa Fe Elementary in North Oakland, Gladys was in a constant search for black history content for her classroom. Countless times it was to the East Bay Historical Society that she turned.

At Emeryville High School, where she taught from 1966 until her retirement in 1975, she again encountered African American students who knew little about their history. "The black kids hated everything black. They were so ashamed." A few years later, she got a group of young Black Panthers as students. "They were the smartest kids at Emeryville High School. I taught a Negro history class, and they really challenged me. They were the cream of the crop!"

A beneficiary for many years of the work done by the Historical Society, Gladys turned to volunteering for the organization following her retirement. For almost two decades she has served as a trustee on the board that helps govern AAMLO. At ninety-five, she also remains active in the Alameda-Contra Costa chapter of The Links, Inc., an international black women's cultural and educational charity organization; in Alpha Kappa Alpha, the country's oldest black sorority; and with the California Council of Negro Women.

Back in 1950, Gladys and her husband moved from their apartment on West MacArthur in Oakland to the newly opened Parchester Village housing development in Richmond. Forty-seven years later, they sold their home and moved to El Cerrito, where Gladys, recently widowed, lives today.

You Want to Be Careful

I was born in Boynton, Muskogee County, Oklahoma on November 16, 1910. I'm the eleventh of twelve children. My father's mother was white, his father was black. Both of his parents were ministers, and they were very strict. My father was a genius. He became a lawyer and even helped to train lawyers. The white people loved him—though he was never allowed to become a judge. He was also a surveyor and a cartoonist. He raised cattle and loved flowers. My mother, who was part Indian and a native of Oklahoma, was smart, too. She was a teacher, and she owned land, acquired because of her Indian heritage. We had a garden and raised cattle and chickens. When the Depression hit, the banks went under and my father lost his money. It just destroyed him.

I was in college at the time. After high school, I went for two years to Spelman College in Atlanta. But with the Depression, it was too hard for my father to both send me money and take care of the family, so I came back home. I'd gotten a teaching credential after the two years, so I was able to find a job teaching school to help the family. I went to Spelman over three more summers, then I finished at Langston University in Oklahoma over another summer and through their evening program. Langston was the only college in Oklahoma that admitted black kids. I got my degree in 1941. Altogether, I taught for twelve years in Oklahoma, before I came to California.

I first came to Oakland in 1942. My fiancé, John Daniel Jordan, had been drafted and was stationed at the Presidio in San Francisco. He said, "I think I'm going to be sent overseas, so why don't you come out to see me before I leave?" At that time you didn't just leave home like that; but my parents liked the young man, and they said, "OK, but you want to be sure to be careful."

Where We Weren't Allowed to Live

I came out here by bus, through Los Angeles. They'd stop for food along the way, but we black people would not be served. We'd go into restaurants and they'd serve anybody else but us. We made some friends on the bus, and one of the Caucasian girls went in and got food for us. We would see signs that said "Whites only." I thought to myself, "And I'm leaving Oklahoma, which is supposed to be so segregated!"

People who had moved to Oklahoma from Mississippi or Texas used to tell us that where they came from, if you met a Caucasian on the sidewalk you'd have to get off and let them pass by. In Oklahoma, when I was growing up, discrimination wasn't that bad. It was minimal because most of our parents were educated. They were doctors or lawyers. If they were farmers, they were good farmers. A lot of them inherited land. Black people could inherit land in Oklahoma, and if they found oil on

Those who wished to reside outside of West Oakland began to seek vacant lots upon which to build their own houses. One of these, the first black fireman in Oakland, made a purchase on Broadway Terrace in the late thirties. Even so, a white friend "fronted" in the purchase just to obtain the property. When the . . . owner attempted to move in, a wealthy white neighbor tried to buy him out. When this attempt failed, his house was fired upon and friends had to be called upon to stand guard. Another black Oaklander having bought a house on Manila Avenue was advised to post a twenty-four hour guard.

Class Aspects of Residential Development and Choice in the Oakland Black Community

your land, you became wealthy.

Discrimination against blacks in Oakland was horrible. When I moved here, we could not go downtown and sit at the Long's Drugstore counter and eat. We were refused service. If I was in a store waiting to be helped and a white person walked up to the counter, she'd be helped first. We would drop friends off to work as maids at houses in neighborhoods where we weren't allowed to live. There were no black people working on streetcars. Years later, I took the first course they gave at Cal on black history. That's when I first saw how one of the encyclopedias depicted black people as animals with tails. This was the impression people had of us!

When I arrived in Oakland, the outstanding black people here were the railroad men. They owned their homes, they had the best jobs. The men were polished—they *had* to be to work as porters. My fiancé's aunt's husband was a railroad man. They found me a place to stay. We had a formal wedding in her home, on February 7, 1943, before my husband shipped out that spring.

I got a job at the Oakland Naval Supply Depot. Even though I had a college degree and a teaching credential, they wouldn't let me work in the main building. Instead they assigned me to the graveyard shift as a time keeper. I worked there from 1942 to 1948.

In 1948, a friend of mine from church and his brother—they were from Texas—had been hired as teachers at McClymonds High School. He encouraged me to apply for a teaching position. He also helped me get my temporary credential from Sacramento. (I later earned a master's degree in education from UC Berkeley.) I was hired to teach at Tompkins Elementary, at the foot of Seventh Street in West Oakland.

In Oakland, they had a saying that the hills schools were different from the schools in the flatlands. The books our kids got were the ones the hill schools didn't want anymore or got rid of due to overuse. Or they'd put books in storage and wouldn't let us use them. But the faculty at Tompkins was integrated, and some of the teachers there who lived in the hills helped us. They said, "You want some books? We'll get them for you."

I started at Woodrow Wilson Junior High [which became Carter Middle School] in September 1950. I think that there were probably no more than five black students. Year by year the number increased dramatically, to the point that when I graduated there was a sizable number of black students there. I think I was kind of on the front end of a wave in all three schools I attended–Longfellow, Woodrow Wilson, and Oakland Technical High School. When I began each school, there was a small number of minority students, be they black, or to a lesser extent, Hispanic, or Asian. By the time I graduated from each one, there was a pronounced increase.

Ray Raineri

Validating Blackness

Tompkins School, circa 1955. *Courtesy of the Oakland History Room*

When I started teaching at Tompkins, there were only sixty black teachers in all the Oakland schools. There was next to nothing in the way of materials at the school administrative building—what was called the "White House"—about black culture that I could show my kids. And there were no other places locally—no library and very few publications—that provided this information. I complained—*all* of us black teachers complained.

In the late 1940s, there was no coalition of black people, *per se*. Everyone was doing things on their own or in small groups. We just didn't have the organization, and so the black community was fragmented. A handful of people who were concerned about the lack of cohesiveness among black people here, and in California in general, decided to do something about it. They came together with the goal of putting out information about African American—we called it Negro then—culture and history. Some of the people involved were Jesse and Marcella Ford, and Ruth and Eugene Lasartemay. They were all older than me—I was in my thirties, and they were maybe ten years older. But they all had children, so they knew firsthand that their kids were not getting this kind of information in school.

Eugene Lasartemay, 1973. *Courtesy of the Oakland History Room*

The Lasartemays had a big home in Berkeley. Mr. Lasartemay was from Hawaii. When he came here he was discriminated against, and it really bothered him. Marcella and Jesse lived on Apgar, not far away from where I lived on West MacArthur. We met through the church. We both were in education, though Marcella wasn't teaching at the time. They were all intelligent, aware people.

They began by clipping newspaper articles—especially Marcella Ford. The *Crisis*, which had been started by W. E. B. Dubois in New York, was one of their sources. The

Oakland was a segregated society. The churches for the most part were segregated. The first black church in Oakland was the Shiloh African Methodist Episcopal Church, which later became the First AME Church. It still exists, near Telegraph and MacArthur. Beth Eden Baptist Church was one of the first black Baptist churches, and it still exists.

The work force, for the most part, was not integrated. The unions shut out black workers, except during a brief period during World War II, when blacks worked in the shipyards. But after that, the unions shut out blacks again. During the post-war period up until the 1960s and 1970s, it was hard for blacks to find work.

Don Hausler

Chicago Defender, and the *California Voice*, which came out weekly and was published in Oakland, were others. They would cut out whatever they thought was of interest. What was most important to them was validating blackness. They wanted kids to feel proud of who they are, to have models of what to look forward to in life. They compiled stories about black inventors and other black people who had distinguished themselves in some way. The group would meet periodically in each others' homes to discuss the material. The Lasartemays were the ones that had the room, so they kept everything, organizing and storing things in boxes.

Marcella Ford, circa 1935. *Courtesy of the Oakland Heritage Alliance*

First Storefront

After this had gone on for some time, the Lasartemays and Fords started the East Bay Negro Historical Society in 1965. The other founders involved were E. Harold Mason, Madison Harvey, and Morrie Turner. In 1970, the Historical Society officially incorporated, and not long after that, they moved into their first office, a little storefront on the corner of Grove and 37th Street. I believe it had been a beauty parlor, run by a black person—you could still see the booths in the back. It was unoccupied, and they got permission to use it.

The front part of the storefront was used by the Historical Society for displays. The back was used for storage. The Lasartemays would display material for a week or so, then take it down, store it in boxes, and then put up a new display. The founders pooled their money to cover whatever expenses they had. Nobody got paid, everyone was a volunteer.

The Historical Society was open afternoons, a few days a week. The founders all belonged to churches, and through them they spread the word about the exhibits and

Oakland Tech was the designated high school to provide English to foreign-speaking students. So, there was a wonderful, rich infusion of kids from South America and Asia, joining kids from Oakland's Chinatown, Mexican American kids who had come out of Westlake, a sizable number of Caucasian kids who were fed into the system from Claremont Junior High and to a lesser extent, Woodrow Wilson [renamed Carter Middle School], and a very small number of blacks who came in from Hoover Junior High on West and 31st Street. Kids from Hoover chose to go either to McClymmonds in West Oakland, which was a predominantly black school by the early 1950s, or to Oakland Tech.

Ray Raineri

The East Bay Negro Historical Society is having an open house celebration tomorrow at its new location at 4519 Grove St. . . . The society's library-museum contains a variety of pictures, artifacts and other materials depicting the history and accomplishments of black Americans—politicians, educators, religious figures, inventors, cowboys and miners who came to California during the Gold Rush.

"Both black and white know so little of the history of the black man," said Eugene P. Lasartemay, president of the society. "Our history was purposely omitted."

Oakland Tribune
March 27, 1976

the other material pertaining to African Americans. They tried to make it easy for teachers to use after school. It was open to anybody, but many of the people who used it were teachers or professionals who were looking for this kind of information.

Grove Street

My husband and I had earlier lived in that neighborhood, on West MacArthur, between Market and West. I don't remember if the neighborhood had a name—we just knew it as Grove Street. It was part of a business area that started around West MacArthur and went toward Berkeley. You could go downtown and buy the same kinds of things, but I found them on Grove. We didn't really ever go to Telegraph.

On the adjacent streets were homes where mostly African Americans lived. They were smaller homes that previously had been occupied by Caucasians. The lower part of Grove, from West MacArthur to downtown, is where the really lovely homes for black people were. The houses had all these rooms, and two or three fireplaces. Those houses also had been formerly occupied by Caucasians.

You Need to Go and Join

Over the years, I volunteered for the Historical Society in different ways. I helped cut out articles—anyone who wanted to bring in clippings was welcome. Stamps were two cents each, so I'd buy a hundred stamps and donate it to them. I could type, so I'd go into the storefront to type things they needed. They wanted to put together a mailing list in order to get people involved and let them know we were trying to get this off the ground. Marcella Ford's church was Beth Eden, so she gave us

East Bay Negro Historical Society, Inc
Founded July 2, 1965
AN AFFILIATE OF THE ASSOCIATION FOR THE STU[illegible] OF NEGRO LIFE AND HISTORY, INC., WASHINGTO[illegible] D.C., AND CONFERENCE OF CALIFORNIA HISTORICA[illegible] SOCIETIES.
PRESIDENT Eugene P. Lasartem[illegible]
SECRETARY Elena R. Jordan

EBNHS membership card, 1982. *Courtesy of Gladys M. Jordan*

I worked at the police department with a fellow named Roy Blackbone. I only found out years later that he had been secretary at one point to Langston Hughes. It was Roy who introduced me to the Fords and the Lasartemays. I remember it was on a Sunday after work. I went straight from work to somebody's house in North Oakland. We sat in the kitchen, talking. I was one of the kids of that group. Madison Harvey was the youngest, and I was the next to the youngest. I listened, mostly, because these people were so knowledgeable. I just kept my mouth shut, listened, and learned. That whetted my appetite, and I started to do research on my own.

The Wee Pals strip started in 1965. When I started doing the Sunday page, I was asked to do what is called a dropout panel, which is a part of the comic that is separate and can drop out if needed without being missed. For a while, I kept changing what I did for the dropout. Then it was Black History Week, which used to run from Lincoln's birthday, on February 12th, to Frederick Douglas's birthday, on February 22nd. I thought, "Why not put in some little history about that period?" The response to it was so great, I thought, "Why wait for a special occasion?" And then, "Why have only history about black people? Why not about the accomplishments of other minority people?" And I've been doing that ever since.

I'm sure in those early days that the source of the material for the dropouts came, either directly or indirectly, from the Fords and the Lasartemays and the others who were working with them. Back then, you had to know where to go. This was before AAMLO. There weren't even black bookstores, and you couldn't find anything at the library. So you had to have a source.

Morrie Turner
West Oakland native, syndicated cartoonist, and creator of the Wee Pals comic strip

NEGRO DOCTOR BUYS LOT ON BURDECK DRIVE

Awakened interest in the problem of restrictive covenants has been shown in the hill section during the past few weeks following disclosure in a special article in the magazine section of the Chronicle that an Oakland Negro physician and his wife are the owners of land in a choice residential section area of Montclair hill section.

As a result of several inquiries as to the location of this property, it was learned by the Montclarion that the lot, formerly owned by another Negro physician, Dr. Le Grand L. Coleman, is located in Burdeck, near Butters drive.

According to Mrs. Dewitt Buckingham, the new owner, she and her husband have no immediate plans for building on the unrestricted lot, which is located among restricted lots in the vicinity. At present, Dr. and Mrs. Buckingham and their three-months-old adopted son are living in the home they purchased in the Claremont district of Berkeley over protest of white home owners in the surrounding area. The home and property are covered by a racial restriction as to use.

It was pointed out that no modern covenants prohibit owners from selling to a person of another race. A covenant restricts the use of property only.

The Chronicle's revelation pointed out that M. C. Friel and associates, who are operating a successful business throughout California, will covenant a neighborhood for a fee. This organization renewed restrictions on about 75 per cent of the properties in the area surrounding the Buckingham's homesite in the hill section.

Meanwhile in Washington, D. C., a decision is pending before the U. S. supreme court with respect to the constitutionality of restrictive covenants. Three justices have disqualified themselves.

A department of justice brief urging the court to ban restrictive covenants says if the present trend toward their use continues unchecked "almost all new residential sections of our cities will be barred within 10 or 20 years, from occupancy by Negroes, and to an increasing degree by other groups."

No official explanation has been given for the decisions of three supreme court justices to withdraw from the case, although it was learned that two of them live in areas covered by a restrictive covenant.

Montclarion, February 15, 1948. *Courtesy of Hills Newspapers*

a list of people from there who she thought would be interested. I was a member of Taylor Memorial Church and told the educators there about the organization and added their names to the Historical Society mailing list. I would also tell black teachers in the public schools, "You need to go and join this organization, because they're doing a whole lot to get our history together."

They involved Tarea Hall Pittman, who had graduated from Cal and lived on Grove Street in Berkeley. She'd had a radio program, "Negroes in the News," that was sponsored by local Negro businesses. It was broadcast every Sunday morning, and she would cover anything pertaining to the East Bay Negro community. We all listened to it to find out what was actually going on in our community and to learn about the things that concerned us.

We created a board of trustees and asked a number of people from prominent businesses to serve on it. All this really paid off. By the mid-1970s we had an active membership program. It cost twenty-five cents for children, and twenty-five dollars for a family to join. Life membership was $300.

A Real Museum

The East Bay Negro Historical Society started out to be a library of mostly clippings, but over time they got collections of other things. Ida Jackson, Oakland's first black teacher, gave the organization a lot of artifacts. They have material from William Byron Rumford. Once a year they would have an open house for families to come in and tell about their history.

There were a lot of prominent black businesses here, and there were organizations like the California Council of Negro Women, the Alpha Kappa Alpha sorority, and Alpha Phi Alpha fraternity. Kids growing up here didn't really know that these black businesses and organizations existed; this was the kind of information the group wanted to make available. They contacted local business owners, like the black morticians, or Mr. Flood, who had a printing establishment that was second to none, and Slim Jenkins, who had a night club on Seventh Street. They wanted to collect the histories of these people and how they got started in business—and to get them involved. I don't remember how they recorded this information, but they wanted to put it together to make it available to others.

Around 1982, the Society moved into the Golden Gate Branch Library on San Pablo where there was room to store all the material and to put on displays. Once or twice a week you could go to the library and talk with someone about the collection. Teachers would take their classes there.

In the late 1980s, we realized that we needed to have a real museum. African American families would give us their collections because we were a black organization,

but we had no real museum experience. We also found out that we wouldn't have jurisdiction over our collections if we didn't officially become a museum. We were happy to loan things out, but we didn't want to risk losing them permanently. The Historical Society decided that they had gone as far as they could as a volunteer organization. One of the long-time members, Dr. Lawrence Crouchett, was a professor at Diablo Valley College. He was asked to be the executive director. They got some funding to help pay his salary. When Dr. Crouchett got in there, things really took off. The board knew that they needed leadership, and he provided it.

Some of Dr. Crouchett's priorities were to further develop the membership program, increase fundraising, and get more educators involved. During his tenure, the name was changed from the East Bay Negro Historical Society to the Northern California Center for Afro-American History and Life—NCCAAHL, which reflected the expanding scope of the organization. Eventually, he recruited Robert Haynes as curator. In the early 1990s, we joined with the Oakland Public Library and formed the African American Museum and Library at Oakland—AAMLO. Ever since then, we've been both a library and museum. NCCAAHL is still the parent group of AAMLO, and we do all of AAMLO's fundraising.

Today, AAMLO is in the beautiful, restored library building on 14th Street and MLK. It's a great place for black children—it's amazing what's there. Dr. Crouchett passed before the renovation was finished. A week before he died, he resigned, saying that AAMLO had grown beyond his furthest dreams. ✦

Opening of AAMLO in the Charles Greene Library, February 24, 2002. (l-r) Madison Harvey, Morrie Turner, Rosemary Thurston, Bill Thurston. *Courtesy of Gladys M. Jordan*

Blockbusting occurred in the 1940s and 1950s, when blacks had difficulty buying houses in white neighborhoods. A white activist would buy a house in a white neighborhood and then sell it to a black family. In that way, blacks could move into white neighborhoods. It started in Trestle Glen. But before that time, there were racial covenants which prevented property owners in white neighborhoods from selling not just to blacks, but to Chinese and other minorities. These were legal until the Supreme Court declared them unconstitutional in 1948. But even when you couldn't legally enforce covenants, there was still an understanding that you wouldn't sell to black people, because of the impact it would have on the neighborhood.

In the early 1950s, there was only one black family in my neighborhood—an older couple, on Manila and Cavour. They were on my paper route. I'm not aware of any covenants in my immediate neighborhood, but my understanding was there were covenants still enforced in Rockridge. It was not until the 1960s when the Rumford Housing Act was passed in California that it became illegal to exclude blacks and other minorities from white neighborhoods.

Don Hausler

Donald Hausler

Don Hausler's relationship with the East Bay Negro Historical Society was unusual in that he was one of the few non-African Americans to have worked closely with the organization in the 1980s. On staff at the Oakland Public Library, and with graduate degrees in both history and library science, Don in his spare time devoted the better part of a decade to researching the history of blacks in Oakland. During this period, he completed two manuscripts on the subject, served on the East Bay Negro Historical Society's advisory board, and was a primary researcher for the Society's ground-breaking exhibit and accompanying book, Visions Toward Tomorrow.

Except for his college years in Utah, Don has spent his entire life in Oakland. Born in 1938 on Lawton Avenue, he attended nearby Rockridge Elementary School (now Far West), Claremont Middle School, and Oakland Technical High School. After receiving his undergraduate and master's degrees in history from Utah State University, Don returned to the Bay Area to teach high school.

It was an entry level job at the Temescal Branch Library in 1967, however, that led him to discover his true calling. "When I started working at Temescal, I knew I was in the right place," Don recalls. "I liked the serenity of the building, I liked the work, and I liked the patrons and the people I was working with."

Don went on to have a long career with the Oakland Public Library, earning his graduate degree in library science from UC Berkeley along the way. His assignments at the library included a stint in the Magazine and Newspaper Room at the Charles Greene Library at 14th and Grove (AAMLO's future home), ten years in the history department at the main library, and as manager of several branch libraries. For the twelve years preceding his retirement in 1999, he served as manager of the Lakeview Branch.

Since retiring, Don has continued as an active volunteer with the Emeryville Historical Society, which he co-founded in 1988. In addition to serving as the editor of its quarterly newsletter, he co-authored Emeryville: A Pictorial History, *published in 2005 by Arcadia Press. In 2001, Don was elected to the board of directors of the Alameda County Historical Society.*

Neighborhood Makeup

Where I grew up, on the 5300 block of Lawton Avenue, I think there was only one Italian family. On the 5200 block, it was mostly Italian, and on Boyd, there were a lot of Italians. Some blocks were probably, 75, 80, 90 percent Italian. The closer you got to Telegraph, the more Italians there were.

Rockridge Elementary School had a 100 percent white student body. Claremont

Jr. High (the old building that they tore down), when I was there from 1950 to 1953, was also 100 percent white. When I was at Tech High from 1953 to 1956, the school was about 25 percent black. I knew only one Mexican kid there, and a few Chinese. At that time, there were several trade courses, like wood shop, auto shop, and metal shop, but many of the white kids were in the college prep courses. Except for typing class, I didn't have one black student in any of my classes. I don't think there were any black teachers. There was a lot of resentment among black students; they felt that they were kind of left out.

Tech High orchestra, 1950. *Courtesy the Oakland History Room*

When I was about 16, I got a job at the Temescal Pharmacy on Telegraph delivering prescription drugs in the neighborhood, on both sides of Telegraph. I went all over on my bike, going as far as West Street, and delivered prescriptions to a lot of elderly Italian women. I don't know what the exact racial composition of the neighborhood was west of Grove Street at that time, but there were a lot of white people still living there. South of MacArthur was a black neighborhood; north of MacArthur was still mostly Italian, still white. I assume that changed in the 1960s and 1970s. By the 1980s it was largely a black neighborhood.

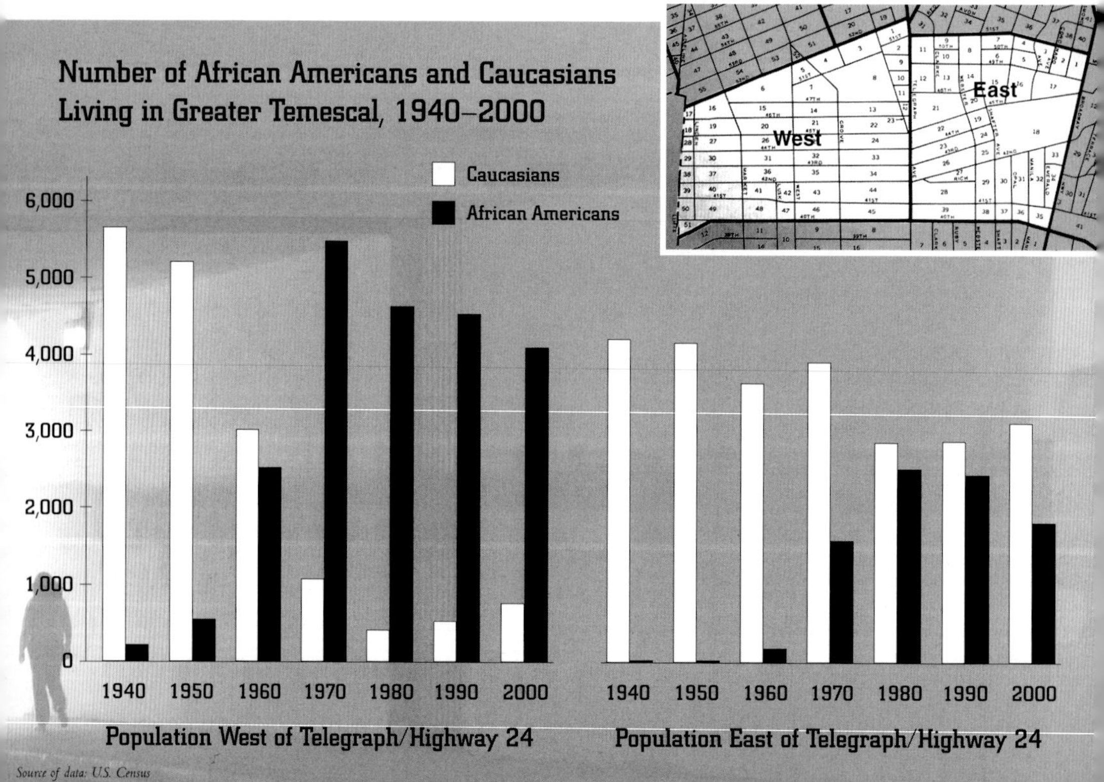

Number of African Americans and Caucasians Living in Greater Temescal, 1940–2000

West

East

Caucasians

African Americans

6,000
5,000
4,000
3,000
2,000
1,000
0

1940 1950 1960 1970 1980 1990 2000

Population West of Telegraph/Highway 24

1940 1950 1960 1970 1980 1990 2000

Population East of Telegraph/Highway 24

Source of data: U.S. Census

Theresa Brooks: I was working in Berkeley when we were looking for a home to buy. There was some construction going on on Claremont, so we had to detour. I think it was because they were building the Grove-Shafter Freeway. Not knowing the neighborhood that well, I wound around and around, trying to get to Highway 17 and out to 98th Avenue, where we were living. Somehow I came down Shafter and made a turn. That's when I saw the sign in the yard on Webster. I took down the number and got home to talk to my husband about it. We came over and looked at the house. Everything just fell into place; we bought the house. That was 1967.

Frederick Brooks: Since we've been living here, we've been blessed. No one, of any creed or color, ever harassed us. We always got along. When we moved from Webster around the corner to 44th Street, people were almost in tears. "Mr. Brooks, don't leave. Mrs. Brooks, we hate for you to leave."

Theresa and Frederick Brooks
Temescal homeowners, 1967–2005

Grove Street Storefront

It was in either 1979 or 1980—I'd just completed my master's degree in library science and was working in the history department at the main library—when I was told that I should tour the East Bay Negro Historical Society, along with some other libraries. That's when I first met Eugene Lasartemay.

At that time, they were in a storefront on 45th and Grove. From what I remember, that area was run down. This was after the completion of the Grove-Shafter Freeway, and I think that it had had a dramatic impact on the neighborhood. Originally there had been a commercial strip there, with several retail storefronts. But by the early 1980s, a lot of those storefronts were vacant. That's how Mr. Lasartemay was able to rent it—it had been vacant, and probably the rent was cheap, too.

Mr. Lasartemay said the store had been a cleaners. You walked in the front door, and there was a counter on the right. If it had been a cleaning establishment, that was the original counter where the cash register had been. There were a couple of stairs leading down into a sunken area, but it was really just one big room. There were photographs on the wall that were mounted—just glued on cardboard and then the cardboard was nailed onto the wall.

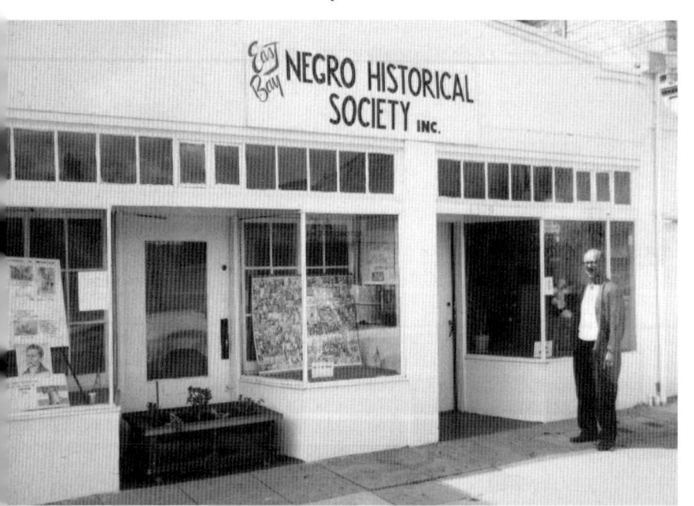

Eugene Lasartemay, on opening day of EBNHS storefront at 4519 Grove, March 28, 1976. *Courtesy of the African American Museum and Library at Oakland (AAMLO)*

It seemed like they were trying to cover the United States, and civil rights, in general. There was also some local history mixed in. There was an exhibit of African artifacts that was in a little roped-off area. People had donated a lot of material and artifacts, and Mr. Lasartemay was trying to display everything, although not all of it fit together. The exhibit, for the most part, was permanent.

I think it originally was open maybe two or three days a week, for a few hours in the afternoon, when classes would sometimes visit. They also held an event every year during Black History Week, which later was expanded to a month.

CITY HALL • 14TH AND WASHINGTON STREETS • OAKLAND, CALIFORNIA 94612

Office of the Mayor
Lionel J. Wilson
Mayor

PROCLAMATION

TO: THE CITIZENS OF OAKLAND

WHEREAS, The African culture both in Africa and elsewhere as it evolves is regaining its ascendancy among world civilizations; and struggle depicts the Black spirit and Black experience in the United States; and

WHEREAS, Alex Haley, with his book ROOTS, makes a unique and essential contribution to the world's understanding and appreciation of Black Culture and History in the United States; and

WHEREAS, Our children must know of the stubborn resistance of Kunta Kinte to the attempts to force him to assimilate a European language and culture; the inspired ingenuity and divine courage which kept Harriet Tubman's Freedom Train moving throughout the land; and the uncompromising opposition to slavery of Frederick Douglas and Sojourner Truth carrying the passed torch of struggle to free the minds of a nation; and unprecedented and audacious vision and ambition of Marcus Garvey for Black people; and

WHEREAS, In the words of W.E.B. DuBois, "The mystic spell of Africa is, and ever was, over all America. It has done her hardest work, inspired her finest literature, and has sung her sweetest song";

NOW, THEREFORE, I, Lionel J. Wilson, as Mayor of the City of Oakland, do hereby proclaim the month of February 1983 as "BLACK HISTORY MONTH", and invite the citizens of our City and our neighbors near and far to join with the East Bay Negro Historical Society in recognition and celebration of Black History so that we may truly be together.

Sincerely,

Lionel J. Wilson

Lionel J. Wilson
MAYOR

Discovering Local Black History

Eugene Lasartemay, 1976. *Courtesy of the Oakland History Room*

I noticed several photographs on the wall which suggested that Oakland's black community dated back to the 19th century. There were at least one or two photographs that dated as far back as the 1860s.

I went back to the library and started looking around to see what I could find on the subject of Oakland's black history, and whether anyone had ever written about it. I looked at Delilah Beasley's *Negro Trailblazers of California*. Over a period of time, I kept doing more research and finding more stuff. And I'd go back to Mr. Lasartemay to try to find out what he had on the subject in all of those files that were in their storefront. Over a period of time I established a relationship with him. That was how I got involved in researching local black history.

Eventually I met everyone who was on the board. Mrs. Lasartemay was the archivist. She would often be behind the counter, in an area where there were two or three filing cabinets. She'd been an active member of the Beth Eden Baptist Church and the church historian. She'd written an account of the church, which I interviewed her about, and the churches that splintered off from Beth Eden around the turn of the century. She knew a lot about that, and about early black history in Oakland. But she was very reticent—she didn't talk that much. Mr. Lasartemay did all the talking.

He was always very kind and gracious. He made you feel at home and was always helpful. He was almost a friend, over a period of time, and was real supportive of what I was doing. I enjoyed working with him.

Mr. Lasartemay was completely devoted to the East Bay Negro Historical Society. He once told me that he had the history of Beth Eden Baptist Church under his bed, because he didn't have room for it anywhere else. He liked to speak to groups on black history, which he did often, and he was an eloquent speaker. He was president of the organization for decades. You have to give him credit for what he accomplished, for his commitment. He wasn't making money—it was *costing* him money. It was a sacrifice on his part to donate his time and his money and his energy. For a long time there probably wasn't that much recognition, either.

Marcella Ford, "Resource Officer," on opening day of EBNHS's storefront museum and library, 4519 Grove, March 28, 1976. *Courtesy of the African American Museum and Library at Oakland (AAMLO)*

Growth of the Organization

In the early 1980s, Lee White, who was the director of the Oakland Public Library, became interested in the East Bay Negro Historical Society. She made an arrangement whereby the Historical Society would occupy the north side of the Golden Gate Library on San Pablo, where there had been a children's room. Library staff moved all the books out and moved the East Bay Negro Historical Society into that part of the building. There was a meeting room in the basement where they held meetings and lectures. There was a storage area in the basement, too. The operation of the Historical Society completely changed after they moved to Golden Gate.

Lawrence Crouchett, who came in as executive director in 1988, saw the potential of the East Bay Negro Historical Society. He wanted to get more funding for it, to expand it, and to find a curator who had museum experience—someone who could catalog all the photographs and put them on the computer, and who could develop professional exhibits. Crouchett had been a college teacher—I think he had a doctorate degree in education. He was on the board of directors of the California Historical Society, and he had a lot of contacts.

He was also very persuasive. He was the one who hired Robert Haynes as museum curator. There weren't many black professionals who were trained in that discipline. Robert Haynes, I think, had been working at the Oakland Museum. He was good, he was smart, and he knew what he was doing. He developed a permanent exhibit, and it was done very well. Crouchett told me he was lucky to find Robert Haynes and have him commit himself to the organization. Overnight, everything kind of exploded.

I remember Mr. Lasartemay, in the 1980s, would visit schools and give talks about the East Bay Negro Historical Society and local black history. A lot of students would question him about the term "Negro" and whether or not it was an anachronism, and whether it would be more correct to use "African American" or "black." He would tell them the etymology of the word and justify its use, even though some people were offended by it and thought it inappropriate.

Dr. Crouchett thought that the focus of the organization should be northern California—not the world, not Africa, not the United States, but northern California. He didn't like the term "Negro" either. Eventually the name was changed to the Northern California Center for Afro-American History and Life.

They also wanted to find a permanent facility and a bigger home. The plan for the organization's move from the Golden Gate Branch to the Charles Greene Library on

14th and MLK was in the works for a long time. It cost millions of dollars to remodel the Charles Greene Library, which is a big, two-story building. They had to retrofit the building, and there were five levels of stacks of newspapers that they had to take out. To go from that storefront on Grove, which wasn't even 1,000 square feet, to the Charles Greene was remarkable. It's amazing that the East Bay Negro Historical Society survived at all, but now they have a permanent home and it will endure. It just shows how an institution can start out on a shoestring, survive for a long period of time, and eventually flourish. ✦

Gladys Jordan, at the Charles Greene Library during renovation, November 15, 1998. *Courtesy of Gladys M. Jordan.*

Several major savings and loan companies continue to practice discrimination in lending although federal laws clearly forbid such practices.

Because of the often outrageous though covert practices, ghetto residents are "frozen" in their existing housing when they want to improve their homes or move to better neighborhoods.

Mrs. Arlene Slaughter, chairman of the equal rights committee of the Oakland Real Estate Board, disclosed these documented charges while speaking to the League of Women Voters last week.

"In a country where we hear and see a demand for law and order, we find some of the most entrenched institutions are engaged in violation of the law," said Mrs. Slaughter.

Savings and loan companies locate their offices in black neighborhoods, take depositors' money and pay interest on their savings, but when it comes to making a home loan, they are not willing to lend the residents money, even at nine percent, she said.

Montclarion
September 29, 1971

If you were white, Temescal Creek was a place that the "other" people used as a corridor for bad deeds—stealing, hanging out, doing bad things. If you were African American, the creek was seen as this scary place to be avoided because the public realm was, in general, bad. You felt at risk from the powers that be, which were inherently against you because of racism. And so, Temescal Creek became something that nobody wanted around.

Bruce Douglas
Founder, Friends of
Temescal Creek

Temescal Creek

The Community Effort to Preserve Wildness

Map showing Temescal Creek (detail) Sanborn Insurance Map Company, 1932. *Courtesy of the Oakland History Room*

Introduction

Flowing down from the Oakland hills through the flatland communities of Rockridge, Temescal, and Emeryville to San Francisco Bay, Temescal Creek forms one of the largest watersheds in Oakland. Prior to the arrival of the Spanish missionaries, the Huchiun Ohlones relied on the creek for food, fresh water, and spiritual sustenance. Vicente Peralta built his adobe a stone's throw from the creek, near present-day Claremont Avenue. In 1868, the young city of Oakland acquired its first municipal water supply when Anthony Chabot dammed the creek to create Lake Temescal. As the city grew, even greater demands were placed upon the creek and the land along its banks. By the 1960s, decades after Oakland had turned to the Sierra for its fresh water, Temescal Creek in the flatlands had become heavily eroded, squeezed by development, and often used as an illegal dumping ground. Still, except for where it passed under streets and through some properties, the creek remained open and in its natural streambed. It also retained a good measure of wildness to which many, especially children, continued to be drawn.

A heavy winter storm in the fall of 1962 changed all this. As a result of significant flooding along Temescal Creek where it crossed San Pablo Avenue, Alameda County agreed in 1963 to provide flood protection. The Alameda County Flood Control and Water Conservation District (ACFC&WCD) drew up plans to contain the creek, in phases, in an underground culvert (imagine a long, concrete, rectangular tunnel, ten feet across and twelve feet high). Significant culverting from Lake Temescal to Hardy Street was completed in the late 1960s as part of the Grove-Shafter Freeway project. In the 1970s, two stretches in the flatlands were culverted: from Hardy Street to Telegraph Avenue, and from Adeline to San Pablo Avenue. The middle section, from Martin Luther King Jr. Way to Adeline, was completed in the 1980s. Today, virtually the entire creek, from Lake Temescal to the bay, has been buried.

Still flowing beneath our streets, carrying runoff from the hills to the bay, Temescal Creek is now largely hidden and unknown to us. Also little known is the battle neighbors fought to keep the stretch of Temescal Creek from Hardy Street to Telegraph from being culverted. And yet, signs of both remain. The little stream—officially called a "reconstituted creek"—that flows (with water pumped from the culvert) during the summer at Hardy Park, and from Clifton, past the Department of Motor Vehicles (DMV), to Clarke Street, serves not only as a trace of the actual creek that runs in the culvert directly below, but as a legacy to the community effort in the early 1970s to keep the creek open.

East bank of Temescal Creek, behind 5229-31 Miles, 1972. *Courtesy of ACFC&WCD*

Telling the story of that effort, Marian Gatti, whose family home on Claremont backed onto this section of Temescal Creek, describes the creek before it was covered. From her we also begin to understand the tradition of care that her family and others brought to the task of preserving this treasured bit of nature in their backyards—long before the creek restoration movement in the East Bay got underway in the 1980s.

Peter Heylin and Dan deGrassi, who in the early 1970s lived across the creek from the DMV, were at the center of the fight to prevent culverting. From them we learn about the community organizing that took place and the events that eventually led to the creation of the linear park and landscaped reconstituted creek over the culvert. We also "connect the dots" between the neighborhood's need then for open space and the community's recent success in establishing the Rockridge Temescal Greenbelt along this same stretch of creek.

Temescal Creek, Redondo and Clarke Street (looking east), 1972. *Courtesy of ACFC&WCD*

To these stories are added the voice of Bruce Douglas, environmental educator and founder of Friends of Temescal Creek. Running through the chapter like a Greek chorus, Bruce's observations provide a valuable analysis of the various social and environmental factors that led to culverting. They also reveal how research and experience over the past thirty years have led to greater understanding of the effects of culverting—and to alternative approaches to flood control.

As with the community's fight over the issue of the Grove-Shafter Freeway, some of those who fought to keep Temescal Creek from being buried question whether their efforts had been in vain. In contrast to the North Oakland neighborhoods further downstream, however, where most residents wanted the creek culverted and the resulting swath of land used as extensions of back yards, the public open space created along the DMV, at Hardy Park, and at Clarke and Redondo became a treasured community amenity. Furthermore, had that open space not been carved out in 1973, there would be no Rockridge Temescal Greenbelt today. Even the stretch from Hardy to Clifton, fenced off to the public in 1974 but with the hope that someday it would become part of the linear park, is now an accessible and vital link in the Greenbelt.

Admittedly, the reconstituted creek today offers only a hint of the mystery and adventure that once drew children and adults alike to the open, meandering creek. During the summer, however, when the water is pumped up from the culvert, the small, flowing stream can still evoke a magical sense of the natural forces that surround us. In an intensely urban setting, where 50,000 people now share the Temescal watershed, this kind of experience, however subtle, is precious.

The 1960s saw the development of the freeway system. Temescal Creek, located at the closest point directly across the bay from San Francisco, suggested an obvious highway corridor because it offered the gentlest grade up the hills. Within the short span of ten years, the Temescal Creek watershed received acres and acres of concrete. From College Avenue in Rockridge up to Lake Temescal, the entire canyon was filled with the roadbed of Highway 24. A large, tunnel-sized culvert was put in to carry the creek water. All of the earthworks—digging the tunnel, filling the land, and paving the streets—completely changed the hydrology of the creek. A significant amount of ground that had been available to absorb water and release it slowly and carry on the normal functions of a creek was replaced by hard surface that allowed the rain to run instantly down this essentially new drain that was created.

Bruce Douglas
Founder, Friends of Temescal Creek

Marian Gatti

Marian Gatti, born in 1933, lives in the same house on Claremont Avenue where she was raised. "My parents bought the house next door to this one. They built the flats and the duplex, and after I was born, they built this house."

Both of her parents were from Genoa, Italy. Marian's father, Giacomo Passadore, was a garbage man for Oakland Scavenger. "He was there in the early days, when the Scavenger's headquarters were just a block south on Claremont."

Marian grew up with Temescal Creek flowing at the edge of her backyard. As a child, her world was the creek. Even now, when describing the location of places in the neighborhood, things are either "up" or "down"—upstream or downstream—from her home.

Marrying in 1959, Marian and her husband, Raymond Gatti, didn't venture far. Living in a home off Park Boulevard, and later on Chabot Road, the Gattis moved back into Marian's family home after her mother, Regina, died in 1979. By then, despite her efforts to help save it, the creek that she had known and loved for forty years was gone.

Growing Up with the Creek

It was beautiful growing up with Temescal Creek right behind us. We had fun all summer long. We'd build dams right in back, which made it possible for us to swim. The creek got about three feet deep and had fish in it. We caught minnows and what we called suckers, which were about six inches long. There were quite a few in the deep parts, the pockets, which sometimes formed at a bend where the water eroded the creek bed. We'd catch them in my mother's mason jars. We'd make mud pies, and put the minnows on them! It was a lot of fun.

My dad put in retaining walls. We had terraced gardens in back, both vegetables and flowers. We irrigated the garden with water from the creek, using a pump. We grew

Temescal Creek, behind 5442 Claremont, 1972. *Courtesy of ACFC&WCD*

Frog Park, behind 5442 Claremont, 2005

zucchini, cabbage, potatoes, peas, carrots, basil. It was wonderful soil. My parents did that for years and years.

Across the creek, Lefty and Hazel Hermle had built flagstone terraces that were beautiful. Ours were concrete walls, but Lefty laid every stone just so. Other neighbors didn't need to put in any retaining walls. Some had larger backyards that sloped more gently, so they had a beach, almost. There were wonderful trees along the banks—eucalyptus, oaks, palms—and bushes. It was quite varied, all up and down the creek.

Flagstone terraces, behind 5341-45 Miles, 1972. *Courtesy of ACFC&WCD*

The creek was curvy and narrow. We played up and down the creek all summer long. We'd go upstream through the culverts—we called them tunnels—almost as far as Lake Temescal. The other way we didn't go too far, although some kids went down as far as the bay. We had candles, because in those days you didn't have flashlights. We wore shoes, or rubber boots, when we went wading.

Walking upstream, we'd go under Hardy Street. That was the first tunnel. When you came out, there were gardens all around. We'd continue up to the next tunnel at what had been Arbor Drive, which is now covered by the freeway. We'd go by College Avenue, and keep going, past Chabot School. That was as far as we could go, because there were wooden planks blocking the next tunnel.

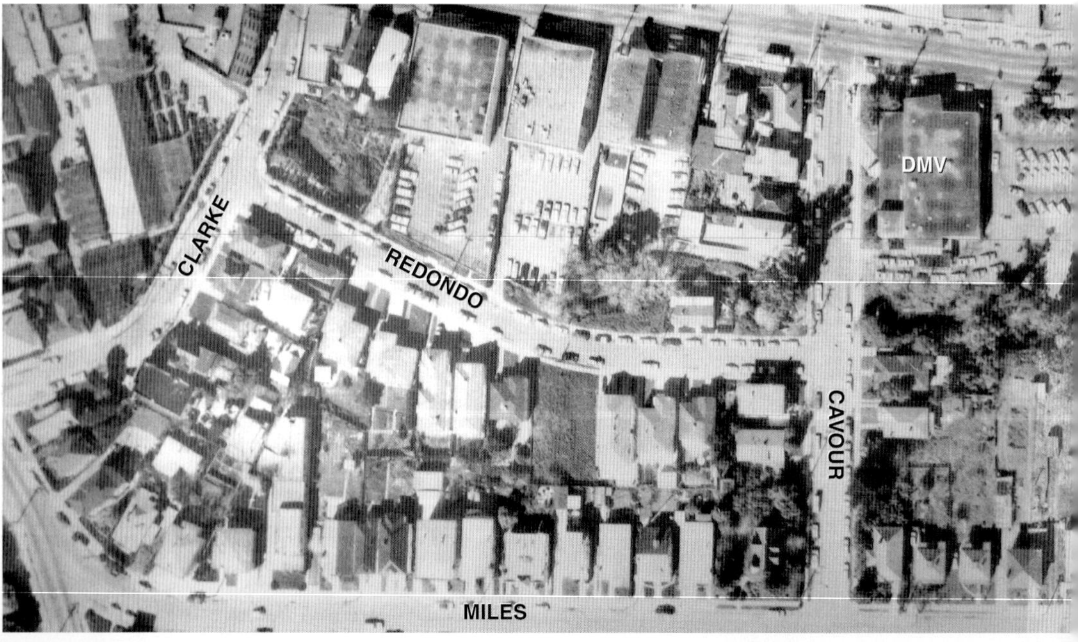

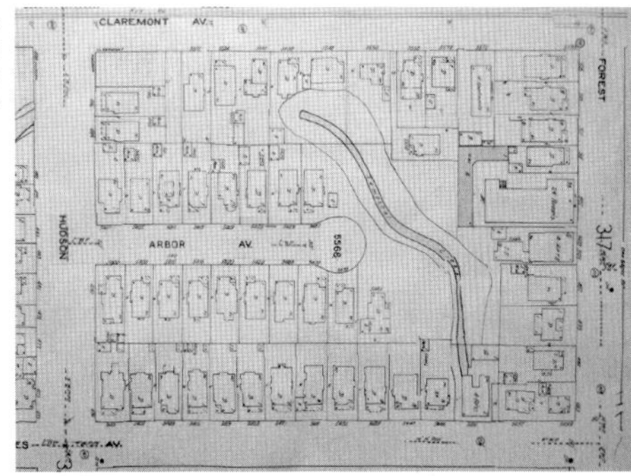

Map (detail) showing Temescal Creek and Arbor Drive, Sanborn Insurance Map Company, circa 1960. *Courtesy of the Oakland Cultural Heritage Survey*

Going downstream, the first tunnel was at Clifton, just down at the end of the block. After the tunnel at Clifton, there was the Kiva Mattress Company. Past that was a residence. We'd follow the creek past where the DMV is now. Back then it was all gardens. The block of Redondo was mostly tunnel. On the other side of Clarke Street, near Telegraph, where McDonnell Nursery used to be, the creek opened up for a little bit before going into another tunnel. There were also tunnels down near the Ligure Club, at Shattuck and 48th Street, and that was about as far as we went. We could have gone further, but we didn't.

Sometimes kids would come up the creek from below Telegraph, and we'd have wars. We'd bombard them with rocks and things. We'd stand up here, where they couldn't see us. They'd come by and boom—we'd start in!

Mallards and geese lived in back of us, which all the kids loved. There was a part in back along the creek that was flat and had no retaining wall. That's where they would nest. My father fed them special grain and leftovers. My parents kept rabbits and chickens in pens for awhile. And they had cats to keep the mouse population down. Everybody had cats.

We always had the sense that the water was clean—until polio set in. That was when I was ten or so. We stayed out of the creek then, because of the fear that polio was transmitted in the water.

Courtesy of ACFC&WCD

In the winter, the creek would swell way up, and it was very dangerous, so we'd stay away from it. You could see garden furniture and other things floating down—whatever people threw in it.

My parents loved the creek. After the winter rains, when the water would come down and erode everything, my father would fill the holes with stones so that kids wouldn't fall into them. We also cleaned the creek. If there were rocks in the way, we'd throw them to the side. If there was any paper, trash, we'd clean it up.

Temescal Creek near Cavour, 1971. *Photo: Dan deGrassi*

In the early 1960s, after I was grown, there was a big flood. Water came up to the platform in our back yard. It brought all this silt, which we had to dig out. The problems got worse from then on.

Later in the 1960s, there were more problems that developed. When the creek rose in the winter, it would fill with all this stuff and block the tunnels. There was a gentleman who had rabbit hutches that got washed away; they blocked the tunnels too. The creek would then back up, and everything else would get caught in it. That was a big reason why they eventually covered the creek.

Covering the Creek

It was around 1970 that I first learned about the plan to culvert the creek. Engineers from the County Flood Control started coming around. They would talk to us and say they were going to cover the creek. All of us were shocked. We didn't want it. We'd had that creek forever. It was very sad. I don't remember any neighbors wanting the creek covered.

We started organizing—and this included neighbors on Miles Avenue—and met at the Columbo Club with one of the environmental groups. There were more than fifty people involved, mostly the old Italians, including my parents—they're all gone now. The ecology group

By 1970, when the freeway was by and large completed, the flows during winter suddenly were much higher than they ever were before. Starting from Hardy Park in the Rockridge area down to the bay, every time there was a large rainstorm, there'd be a huge increase in flow in the creek. By that time, people had built quite a crowded infrastructure right up to the creek, all through the alluvial plain, so every time there was a high flow event, a lot of people's creek banks would get eroded. You also had a lot of really dangerous bridges and culverts.

Bruce Douglas

491 Hardy Street (demolished). *Courtesy of ACFC&WCD*

Same view: former site of 491 Hardy Street.

491 Hardy Street (demolished), and creek culvert and bank. *ACFC&WCD*

Same view: Hardy Park.

Temescal Creek and 5442 Claremont. *Courtesy of ACFC&WCD*

Same view: Hardy Park (5442 Claremont, behind trees).

Barn and terraces (demolished), 5442 Claremont, rear. *ACFC&WCD*

Same view: Frog Park and pump station (5442 Claremont, behind trees).

1972 *2005*

Clifton Street, intersecting Temescal Creek. *Courtesy of ACFC&WCD*

Clifton Street, intersecting the Rockridge Temescal Greenbelt.

Backyard, 484 Cavour Street. *Photo: Dan deGrassi*

DMV parking lot, former backyard of 484 Cavour Street.

Cavour Street, intersecting Temescal Creek (looking south). *ACFC&WCD*

Cavour Street, intersecting Temescal Creek culvert (looking south).

Temescal Creek, along Redondo. *Courtesy of ACFC&WCD*

Reconstituted Temescal Creek, along Redondo.

tried to help us. We saved some trees with their help—oaks, eucalyptus. We'd talk with the engineers, call Flood Control in Hayward.

Barn (demolished), at rear of 5442 Claremont, 1972. *Courtesy of ACFC&WCD*

Across from Frog Park, where the kids now play at Hardy Park, where the big grate is now, there was a beautiful, old horse barn. It was built in the late 1800s and was a historical part of Temescal. It had a hayloft, old boards—it was wonderful. We tried to save that, but they knocked it down.

We just wanted people to take care of their own backyards and not leave the stuff that would block the tunnels. Things were also coming down the creek from higher up, which was also part of the problem. People further up, around College Avenue, all knew about the problem. Word spread.

But, it was out of our hands. The same thing had happened with the building of the freeway—we'd fought that too.

Before the culvert, everyone's property had extended halfway into the creek. They sent appraisers in to buy the land from us that they needed to build the culvert. We

Engineering-wise, what's wrong with culverting as a solution is that it's helping to kill the bay. All of the rain water from all of the streets runs down the storm drains and into the creeks. There is no plumbing system that's separate from the creek to take rain water anywhere, so all of the oil and runoff from people's lawns, and leaf matter from the trees, goes down the storm drains and into the creeks—and ends up in the bay. What they didn't think about in their solution of getting the water out of there quickly, was where the water was going to go. Bruce Douglas

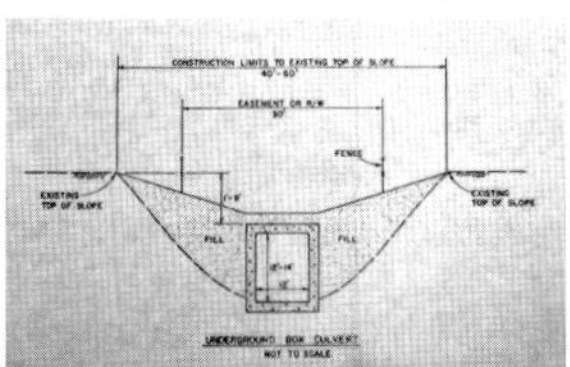

Diagram, culvert cross section. *Courtesy of ACFC&WCD*

Background: Open channel, Temescal Creek, Emeryville, 2001.

were compensated for the land, but not all that well. But, if you didn't take what they offered you, they'd say it wasn't worth much and take your property anyway. It turned out that they overbought, so we offered to buy back some of the land. But they said no to this, too.

When they were building the culvert, my mother's friends—the old ladies—would come from San Francisco. They'd sit on the deck and watch the contractors pour the concrete for the tube. It was an Italian construction company from Hollister, I think. As I recall, the tunnel was ten by twelve feet. It was a mess. It took a couple of years or so, from the time they started. Then they covered the culvert with about five feet of soil—except that they brought in the dirtiest, rottenest dirt, filled with hunks of macadam. Nothing ever grew on it. Once in a while the County would come through to trim some branches. It wasn't beautiful.

They put up fences along our backyards and at the ends of the block for our safety. For the most part, it hasn't been bad over the years, but we've still had trouble with a few people climbing the fence and stealing plants from our backyards.

Along some parts they built the miniature creek, I suppose to give some semblance of what the real creek had been like; but I didn't care about it. There had been the idea back then of creating a park all along where the creek had been. And they wanted people be able to walk from Claremont, right through our property to our back, to get to it. We didn't think that was a good idea.

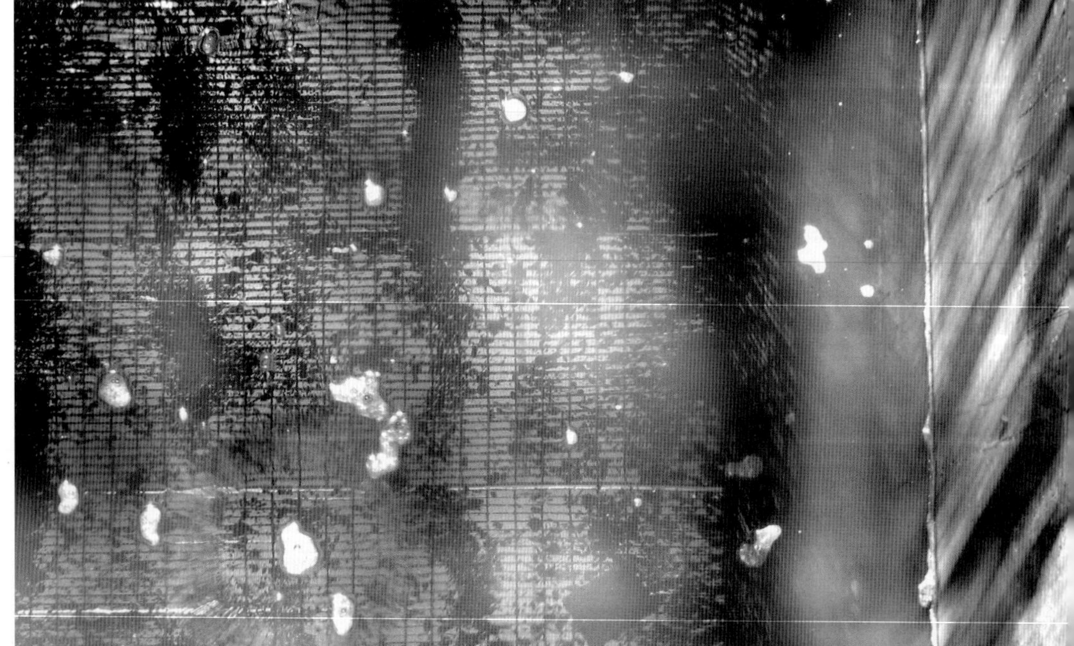

Temescal Creek culvert, seen through access grate, Hardy Park, 2005.

The new Frog Park is a wonderful place for the children, but it's not really for our benefit. At eight o'clock in the morning on the weekends, sometimes as early as seven, there's screaming and crying. But you get used to it. It's fun for them, it's great—darling children, a community effort—but my tenants don't like it. They do maintain the park very well now.

The creek never had to be culverted. There was always damage, but if people had taken care of the creek, this never would have happened. The flooding was caused by people's negligence.

It would be wonderful to have the creek here again as long as it would be safe for kids. It would be a mess, getting that ten by twelve concrete tube out. But, if that could be done, and people were responsible and kept it clean, it would be wonderful. The creek brought birds in—and wildlife. Sometimes a heron would fly in. It was calming to look at. We would lie in bed at night and hear the trickle of the water. It was like being in the country. And the creek brought people together, especially the children. Then all of a sudden it was covered with this horrible dirt. It ruined our lives for a while. It was very stressful for all of us at the time. We were so sad. I'd be one hundred percent for it if we could have the creek again. ✦

If you flush water quickly into the bay, and take with it soil, leaves, trash, oil, fertilizer, pesticides–all these things that come from our yards and streets–and deposit them in the bay, the bay quickly dies. There's a food-production chain in the bay that keeps the organisms in the bay alive. It begins with the bottom of the bay having microorganisms and small invertebrates that produce a lot of food. Creeks that are delivering water quickly to the bay keep the silt suspended in the water and then deposit it in the bay, so that the bottom repeatedly gets covered up. These organisms get buried and have to reestablish a new environment for themselves. In the process, their numbers get severely reduced.

Bruce Douglas

Mouth of Temescal Creek, Emeryville, 2002.

Temescal Creek, off Hardy Street (looking east), 1972. *Courtesy of ACFC&WCD*

Same view: Hardy Park, Rockridge Temescal Greenbelt (looking east), 2005.

Previously, the County Flood Control District had culverted creeks in Oakland and elsewhere, and it seemed that no one much cared. But in the early 1970s you had an interesting dynamic. People were beginning to become concerned about creeks. At the same time, you had a frequent pattern in which many of the people who actually lived along the creek—the property owners especially—were all too happy to see the creeks buried and forgotten.

John English
Oakland city planner, 1961-1978

Peter Heylin and Dan deGrassi

Peter Heylin and Dan deGrassi were both in their late twenties when they met as next door neighbors on Cavour Street. In 1969, Peter had arrived to the neighborhood with his first wife, Mary, determined to take some time off from his corporate career to "become a hippie for a little while."

Dan moved in next door a short time later, and soon both households were part of the close-knit community of residents living on the south end of their block of Cavour, between Temescal Creek and Miles Avenue. Among their neighbors were Mark Monaghan and Pat Shayler, both of whom were on the staff of the then recently formed Ecology Center in Berkeley. As co-director, Mark asked Peter to advise on some matters at the center. It was also through Mark and Pat that Peter and Dan became involved in the effort to save the nearby stretch of Temescal Creek from being culverted.

"Initially, I was drafted by Mark to help straighten out the finances of the Ecology Center," Peter explains. "At the same time, my wife's aunt was one of the two people who led the effort to save the marshlands in Palo Alto. They were all working on me, and I caught the environmental bug."

By then, Peter had gotten a job as assistant vice president in marketing for Lucky Lager in South San Francisco. Before long, he was running the recycling programs at Lucky Lager, implementing a zero waste program for the entire plant. He hired his friend and next door neighbor, Dan, to help out.

"Peter got me into my first recycling job." recalls Dan, "I worked in the back of the Lucky Lager recycling truck collecting bottles and cans." Since 1977, Dan has worked for Santa Cruz County. "I'm now a solid waste planner for the county. I started the curbside program there and virtually all of the recycling that happens in the county. Hopefully, come June, we'll start our first commercial food waste composting collection program. Garbage is my life!"

By 1974, Peter, Mary, and their infant daughter had moved to Canyon, on the other side of the hills, and Peter had come on board full-time at the Ecology Center. "We started a program called ENCORE, which was an acronym for Environmental Container Reuse. We bought used wine bottles, then washed, repacked, and sold them to wineries, in place of new bottles." The project, which had been developed by the Ecology Center as a solid waste demonstration program, eventually was spun off as a private company, which Peter ran until he retired in 2000. Shortly after, he and his family moved from Canyon to rural Santa Cruz County, into a home surrounded by redwoods and overlooking the San Lorenzo River.

Since 1977, Dan and his wife, Laurel, have lived in their Santa Cruz home—also by a creek—where their two children were born and raised.

Living Creekside

Peter: I moved to 484 Cavour Street in the spring of 1969. After I had gotten my MBA from the University of Chicago, I was recruited by Gallo and moved to Modesto. Modesto was terrible, I quit, and my wife and I looked in the East Bay for a place to rent. The two-bedroom house on Cavour was renting for $175 a month, which was a pretty good deal.

Dan: I think it was 1969 or 1970 when I moved to Cavour. I'd graduated from Cal in 1968 and lived in the East Bay—Berkeley, Oakland—for a year or so. My brother's friends found this place—it was a three-bedroom house, between Peter's house and Temescal Creek. At the time, I was working for a social research company in Berkeley.

Garage and driveway, 484 Cavour, 1971. *Photo: Dan deGrassi*

Peter: When we moved in, the creek was open almost the entire way between Hardy Street and Telegraph. A woman who lived on Redondo just below the little bridge that crossed Cavour had a house that was built almost on top of the creek. It had a deck that went right over it—in fact she later became one of the people who really wanted the creek culverted, because it was a problem for her. Below her, a portion along Redondo had already been culverted. On the other side of Clarke Street, the creek went through McDonnell's Nursery, which later became the big bank building, then went into the culvert at Telegraph. It opened up again for a whole bunch of blocks on the other side of the freeway, and on toward Emeryville. We actually followed it once, back when we were trying to save it from being culverted. You could literally go up on a hill in Rockridge and see the route of Temescal Creek by following the line of trees to Emeryville.

There were several houses on the end of the block of Miles and Cavour where we lived. The three houses on Cavour and the three that went up Miles were all owned by the same person, Henry Anderson. On Cavour, nearest the creek, was Dan's house; then my house; then the corner house on Miles and Cavour, where Mark Monaghan and Pat Shayler lived. The next house up Miles is where the Persians were. Next to them was [the rock band] Commander Cody and his Lost Planet Airmen. Asleep at the Wheel lived in their basement for a long time. Then

Backyard, 484 Cavour, 1971. *Photo: Dan deGrassi*

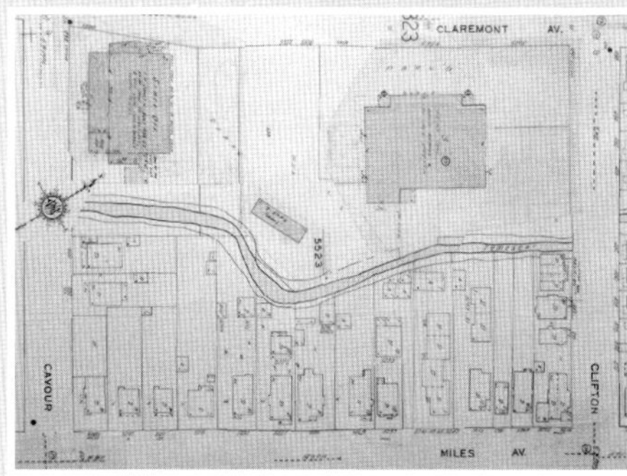

Map (detail) showing Temescal Creek, Sanborn Insurance Map Company, circa 1960. *Oakland Cultural Heritage Survey*

there was a Korean artist, Harry King, and his girlfriend.

Henry Anderson didn't care what we did, because, as he told us, all the houses were going to be torn down to make a parking lot for the DMV.

Dan: The DMV already had a parking lot, but they wanted another, bigger one.

Peter: We took down all the fences that were separating our back yards, and we jointly built a creekside gazebo (with wood pulled out of the Oakland estuary), which we all used. The creek became part of the whole backyard scene, which included community volleyball and lots of barbecuing.

Backyard, 488 Cavour Street, 1971. *Photo: Dan deGrassi*

Dan: Our house sat parallel to the creek. There were a number of overgrown plum trees between us and the creek bank. It was overgrown in a lot of places, and we cleared it a little; but there was also a fence that ran on the side of the house that faced the creek, so we didn't really go down right there all that much. In the communal backyard, the drop from the top of the bank to the bottom of the creek channel was ten feet or so, but it sloped pretty gradually to the creek. There were eucalyptus trees on both sides of the creek, but they didn't dominate.

Peter: The creek was a nice place to hang out; we spent a fair amount of time down there.

Dan: The creek was like your basic urban creek. It had litter and junk in it—broken bottles and old cans—but we'd clean out our little stretch.

Peter: The creek flowed all year round. Where we lived, it had frogs, fish—nothing big. Still, I would have called it a distressed creek. Along the banks in places were these three-foot-long cylinders that were used to shore up the

Temescal Creek and retaining wall, behind 5227 Miles, 1972. *Courtesy of ACFC&WCD*

Safeway, 5354 Claremont, 1972. *Courtesy of ACFC&WCD*

bank. We heard that they were disposed CO_2 canisters that had come from a nearby brewery. The litter I recall was mostly the stuff that blew across the Safeway parking lot and into the creek. I don't remember whether there was a fence behind Safeway, but I could get to Safeway by going through the creek.

Dan: I don't remember the creek ever getting really high, though there might not have been heavy rain years the years we were there. It certainly never went over the banks where we lived.

The First Wave of Organizing

Peter: We first heard about the culverting idea from our neighbors, Mark Monaghan and Pat Shayler, sometime in 1970. Both of them were working at the Ecology Center in Berkeley. They got wind of it, and they invited us all to their place to see if we could do something about it.

At first, I thought the culverting idea was part of the DMV's plan for the parking lot, but that wouldn't explain why they wanted to culvert the whole stretch of it, from Hardy to Telegraph. It turned out that the culverting was being planned by Alameda County Flood Control. It was one of the creeks marked for doom by the very active Flood Control agency at that time. We decided to try to keep the creek from getting culverted.

Dan: Our argument was: the natural environment is something that most people living in an urban setting rarely experience.

A beneficial effect on the quality of Temescal Creek and San Francisco Bay waters will result from the proposed culverting. Creek waters will no longer serve as a convenient conveyor for garbage . . . and other refuse discharged into them, and will, therefore, flow in a cleaner condition, thus providing higher quality water for percolation and the discharging of cleaner water into the bay. In addition, the quantities of mud, silt and debris resulting from the continual erosion along these reaches of the creek will no longer be transported to the lower reaches of the creek and to the bay where they have in the past been deposited. These deposits have caused the need to dredge the creek outfall which results in additional problems associated with disturbance of the Bay waters and disposal of dredge spoils.

Environmental Impact Statement: The Improvement of a Portion of Line A–Temescal Creek, Bissell & Karn, Inc., 1972

Peter: You could hear frogs. There were stories of Vicente Peralta being able to bring his boat up to where the DMV is now! Why would you want to lose this?

Dan: A creek is different than a park, even though both consist of things that are "natural." A creek is a wild place; it moves in its own wild way and in rhythm with the cycles of the seasons. There is in each of us, at some level, a sense of this cycle and thus reflects to us that which we can never leave—our own cycle of life and death, which is wild, beyond our control. Water connects us to this.

Peter: The first public meeting was held at the Columbo Hall on Claremont. Alameda Flood Control came; Betty Ann Bruno, who was running for the City Council from District One, was there; and a whole lot of neighbors. Later meetings were at the Columbo Hall and at another location on Grove Street. There might have been neighborhood meetings below Grove, as well, because there was a stretch of the creek down there that they also wanted to culvert. But our meetings concerned the part of the creek that ran from Hardy Street to Telegraph.

At that first meeting, Flood Control didn't present a proposal to us. Instead, they introduced Irwin Luckman. They said, "We've hired this guy who's president of People for Open Space." Luckman, who was an architect, was going to go study it and come back with something. We thought he might come back with a proposal to leave the creek open.

Meanwhile, we used the Ecology Center, mostly because they had a printing capability, and the staffers had some time to work on the project. They also had files that were pretty extensive and a list of affinity groups whom we could call to get more background information so that we weren't totally clueless when we walked into the meetings with Alameda County Flood Control. We became almost a subcommittee of the Ecology Center, using their assistance when we could.

A natural creek is a big filter system. After rain hits living plants, the water softly reaches the ground and flows through dead leaves and plant roots, stays in the soil, and percolates out slowly. As water flows down the creek, it meanders so any silt gets deposited in the creek: the creek bed is a continual process of depositing and moving silt. A healthy creek is also full of organisms and plants that trap and digest the organic matter that makes it into the creek. The mouth of the creek is a wetland that is able to process a lot of nutrients and turn them into organisms that are useful to the bay ecosystem. With the creek culverted, instead of the bay receiving water processed through its natural system, it receives unfiltered water, full of oil, metals, and other poisonous elements that enter the creek from street runoff. The whole delivery system is disrupted.

Bruce Douglas

The social geography of our area tends to be stratified by elevation. If you look at the map, the major class, economic, and social divisions of society are mirrored as you go upstream, beginning with industry and lower income people. As you climb higher up the watershed it becomes more middle class, and in the headwaters it is upper middle class.

If you were a white person you perceived that there was an element of people–whether spoken or unspoken, racist or not, black or not–to be wary of and to blame for theft and violence. If you were African American, there was this scary threat of being oppressed by a group of people who didn't understand you and didn't want you around. Public places and the outdoors shifted from being a community space to being kind of a war zone where you needed to protect yourself. The creek ran right through the center of all this, and so the creek became something that nobody wanted.

People saw the creek as a social problem and as a physical problem. Property owners along the creek would just as soon have more land to build on. The value of nature in the city no longer seemed to exist. Nature had no place; nature meant manicured parks, lawns, and flower gardens. A wild thing like a creek, a riparian zone, wild animals in the city–these just weren't part of people's thinking.

Bruce Douglas

Betty Ann Bruno came down in favor of keeping the creek open, so there was the possibility of getting the Oakland City Council's support. My major in business school had been marketing and research, so we surveyed the neighborhood, because we knew statistics were important.

Flood Control had never run into this. The people they'd dealt with on the other creeks they'd worked on basically said, "Yeah, that creek is a problem—culvert it!" I think they were surprised by us.

At the same time, Flood Control used the fear of access—of undesirable types coming up through the creek to break into people's homes—to scare the older neighbors into wanting the culvert. They could then go back and say, "Hey, we went to the neighborhood and took a hand vote. Everyone who *counted* said, 'Bury it,' and all these hippies just said leave it open." That's an overgeneralization, but not much of one.

One of our concerns was that the culverting would result in trees along the creek not getting their water and dying. At one of the meetings, one woman said, "When you do this culvert, can you take out the trees, too? I hate them—having to rake, the eucalyptus stink." So there was this older neighborhood crowd that didn't see any value in the creek at all.

There were also a number of older Italians who were on our side. I don't think we would have gotten anywhere if we hadn't had some support from the so-called establishment neighborhood.

Dan: I think it was a generational thing. It was the early 1970s. The environmental movement was starting to flower. People our age were more nature oriented, whereas people in their sixties or seventies weren't. I don't think that trees and creeks and water meant that much to them.

Peter: I talked to old man McDonnell, who was one of the people wanting to culvert the creek. His nursery had been flooded a couple times, before we were there. I think he felt he could sell his property to the bank for more money if the threat of flooding wasn't there. [American Savings subsequently bought the property and built a branch office on the site.] He was a kindly old man, but again, much the same as for the neighbors who were worried about access by thieves from the open creek, he basically was looking out for his own economic interests.

Maybe we didn't make the argument well enough, that this creek was actually an asset. That was the argument we were trying to make.

The Compromise

Peter: Irwin Luckman essentially was the guy who put the dagger in the back of any hope we had for preserving the open creek. He was the one who came back with the proposal for a reconstituted creek.

He presented it as, "There is no other option that they will go for. This is the best I could do, and I really bloodied myself getting this much for us. As you can see, there's support in the neighborhood for the culverting, there's damage that's been occurring along the creek because of flooding in the past."

Our answer was, "Well, the reason for the flooding is that they built these culverts in the first place."

Dan: He was an old-school environmentalist, a fifties or sixties environmentalist. His idea of environmentalism was "Parks are cool," not the environmentalism that really came to define the term.

Landscape plan for the proposed linear park, Irwin Luckman, 1972. *Courtesy of ACFC&WCD*

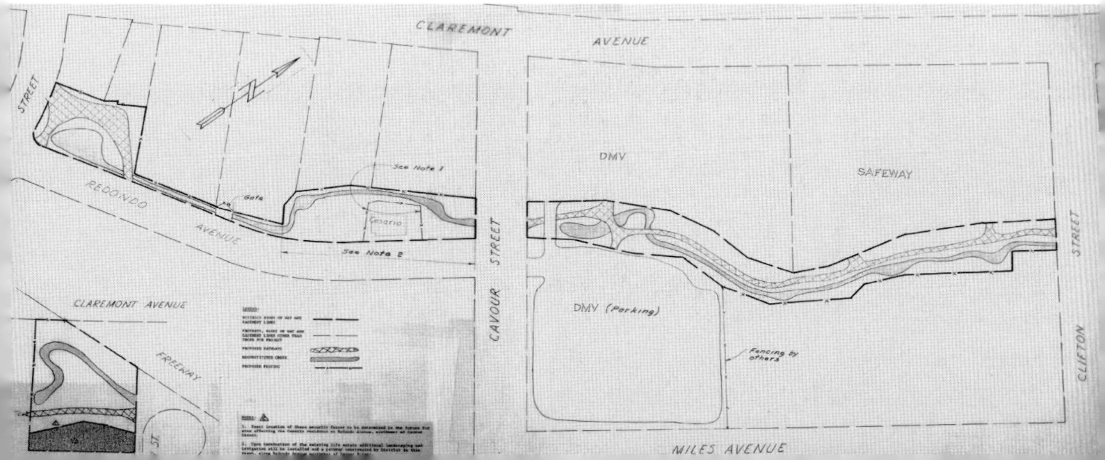

Peter: Luckman argued that the reconstituted creek was going to be the best of both worlds. This guy, who was president of People for Open Space, an architect, and on the payroll of the Alameda County Flood Control, said, "You young people have to learn how to compromise."

Shortly after that, we all got the boot from our homes. By the end of 1971, we were gone from the neighborhood, and as far as we knew, the reconstituted creek was a done deal.

The Second Wave of Organizing

Peter: There actually were two different waves of groups trying to save the creek. The first was us, while we lived in the houses. A year or so later—late 1972 or early 1973, maybe, because by then all of our houses had been demolished, and I was living in Canyon—yet another group came up, trying to save Temescal Creek. That's the group that included Alphonse Durieux and Annette Drujon, who lived up on Clifton, and other neighbors. This vision—the second wave—was not only to leave the creek open, but to create a park where the DMV wanted its new parking lot and to put their parking lot up on Hardy Street, under the freeway.

When we left the neighborhood, we figured the parking lot was a *fait accompli*. But back when all of us were living there, we realized what an asset this big back yard could be to the neighborhood. The six houses had used it as a park, so, given that the houses were going to be leveled anyway, we could see very easily how it could be made into a community park for the older Italian folks and the other people in the neighborhood. It would be wonderful for them! So, moving the DMV's parking lot up under the freeway at Hardy Street, where there was plenty of room and was not that far away, seemed like a great idea.

This next Temescal Creek group definitely had a lot more neighborhood support.

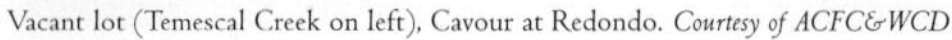
Vacant lot (Temescal Creek on left), Cavour at Redondo. *Courtesy of ACFC&WCD*

DMV parking lot (reconstituted creek on left), Cavour at Redondo.

Rpt #3

Final W.S. calc.

10'×12' RCB Vic. Telegraph
to below Shattuck

℄ Sta. 121+00 to Sta. 128+94.95 L = 794.95' (℄ calc)

℄ D.S. = 86.5' (Set) ℄ U.S. = 97.87 S_o = .0143

Q_{25} = 1660 cfs , Q_{100} = 2150 cfs (See sheet 2c Hydrology calc.)

1) Calc. D_n for Q_{25}

$$K' = \frac{1660 \times .015}{464 \times .1195} = .45$$

D/b = .69 , D_n = 6.9' , A = 69□' , V = 24.1 '/s, h_v =

$$F = \frac{24.1}{(32.2 \times 6.9)^{1/2}} = 1.62 \therefore \text{Flow supercritical}$$

2) Determine D_n in existing Arch

S_o = .0112 (See P-266) Use n = .016

$Ar^{2/3}$ full = 101.0 × 1.925 = 194.5

a_1 = 6.5×9.5 = 61.7□'
a_2 = .393 × 100 = 39.3□'
101.0□'

r = 2.67

P_1 = 13.0+9.0 = 22.0'
P_2 = 15.9' = 15.9'
37.9'

R=5'
6.5'
9.0'
Existing Arch
See FB 12-11

$$\text{Req'd } Ar^{2/3} = \frac{1660 \times .016}{1.486 \times .106} = 168.9$$

∴ Culvert flows less than full

$Ar^{2/3}$ flowing to springline:

$$Ar^{2/3} = 61.7 \times \frac{(2.80^{2/3})}{1.987} = 122.8$$

Engineering Calculations, Temescal Creek culvert, 1965. *Courtesy of ACFC&WCD*

> **The chosen solution was to put in a concrete culvert. Tax dollars were used to fix the problem. But what happened was that tax dollars were spent to "improve" the local area–where the taxes were supposed to be invested–but the actual income and profits were made by companies that had no connection to the community. The flow of money was out of the community. If you compare culverting as a way to solve flooding, pollution, and social problems with a program that involves getting the neighbors to take ownership and improving the banks of the creeks, and working with the property owners, then there was a significant lost opportunity for tax dollars to enrich the people in the community directly.**
>
> Bruce Douglas

Whereas our first group focused on the creek, they wanted the creek left open *and* the park. That's when the issues got linked. By then, the compromise that Irwin Luckman came up with had pretty much been adopted by Alameda County. The second wave was trying to fight that fight over again, but, if they failed in that, then they would settle for a new park by the DMV that would include the little, reconstituted creek.

This group also worked with the Ecology Center, which is how we came back into the picture. Just so you get how all this ties together, the Ecology Center was founded in 1968. It was started by a bunch of environmentalists who knew nothing about running a business. They had some wealthy folks who were dumping money into the organization; meanwhile, the Center was bleeding cash. In 1969, when we met Mark Monaghan living in the corner house at Miles and Cavour, he already was an Ecology Center staffer. Monaghan found out I was a business executive and asked me if I could come and give them some business help. A year later I was chairman of the board.

Dan: I started working at the Ecology Center in 1972. I'd been gone for ten months in 1971, and came back around Thanksgiving. All of our houses were gone by then. On February 13, 1972, the day I turned 26, I got my induction notice. Mark Monaghan worked at the Ecology Center doing his alternative service as a Conscientious Objector. So, I said, I'll do that too.

Peter: And I go before the Selective Service Board to testify that Dan's really a CO!

Dan: That's how I got involved in the creek at that point, because I worked on land-use issues—Sunol Park and Temescal Creek—at the Ecology Center.

Hand-made sign, Miles and Cavour, early 1973.
Photo: Alphonse Durieux

Peter: The park idea had a benefit to the neighborhood that the previous, just-save-the-creek group didn't have. People really got behind it. Neighborhood support extended all the way past Shafter and up toward College.

Peter Heylin, with press at demonstration held on the contested vacant lot, Cavour Street, early 1973. *Photo: Alphonse Durieux*

By the time the second wave came around, the veneer of trust had been wiped away. Two people in that group served as *pro bono* attorneys. I can't remember if it had just been a threat or if there actually was a legal action, but this was a much more politically savvy group. It tried to get the intervention of the Oakland City Council and got the neighborhood riled up. We organized a demonstration—which was covered by every TV station—on what's now the big DMV parking lot. We also had a benefit for the Creek at Ashkenaz [dance and music center in Berkeley].

Maybe forty people would show up at meetings. A lot of them were older neighbors who still felt that the people from the other side of the Grove-Shafter Freeway could use the creek as an access to get into their backyards and rip them off, and that if it was culverted, they wouldn't have to worry about that. I'm sure there were exceptions, but it was still basically the young people wanting the creek open and a lot of the older Italians in the neighborhood wanting it gone.

The DMV hadn't been in on the first battle to keep the creek open. Back then, they'd said, "We'll go along with whatever you folks want to do." This time, the DMV said there wasn't any room for discussion about changing the location of their parking lot—that putting it at Hardy Street was too far from the DMV for people to walk.

There was more pressure brought on. As I recall, John Sutter, who had come onto the city council, wrote some letters. We pushed as hard as we could.

Compromise Redux

Peter: The compromise that was proposed was putting the park under the freeway. The creek was wider up there at Hardy Street than it was next to where we had lived. Originally, there hadn't been any plans to put a park there; it was essentially to be what they called a "lift

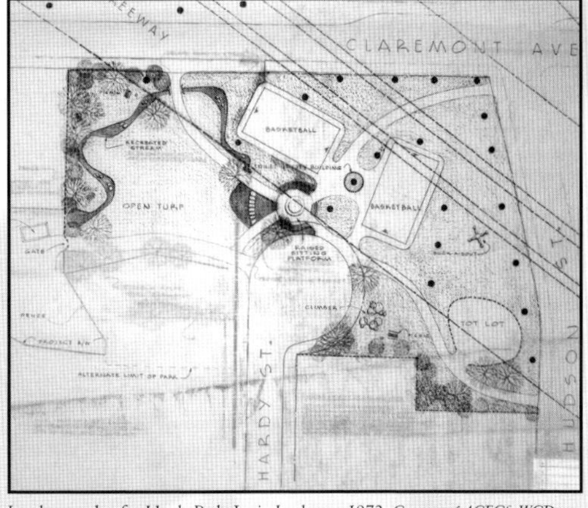

Landscape plan for Hardy Park, Irwin Luckman, 1972. *Courtesy of ACFC&WCD*

Sign, Claremont Avenue below freeway, 1973. *Photo: Alphonse Durieux*

station," a box that housed the pump to bring up creek water for the reconstituted creek.

When they proposed the Hardy Street site as an alternative—we called it Troll Park—we went out and took carbon monoxide readings—whatever comes out of cars—under there. The levels were off the charts. We said, "Do you really want your kids hanging around under there with all this stuff coming off the freeway?" Apparently, it wasn't an issue.

Defining the Loss

Dan: I think that the human species has a connection to the natural world that runs deep. Creeks have water in them. We're 98 percent water, we have an affinity to it. I don't know if *everybody* loves nature, but for most people, there's something that happens. Water flowing gives you some kind of spiritual connection, whether you're aware of it or not. It gives you sustenance. Just the continuity of that helps you as a finite, impermanent, mortal being transcend your mortality. For me, all this happens. Usually, I'm not even aware of it, but it's there.

Peter: There's a unique danger in going down to a creek that's raging in the middle of January, with your mother yelling at you, "Get away from there, you're going to fall in and die!" There's a unique thrill to that kind of experience. In urban areas, where just about every bit of nature has been paved over, we're denying people these experiences.

It was agreed that there would be public access to the reconstituted creek between the DMV and its parking lot. There was some question about whether it would continue behind the Safeway through to Clifton Street. Along Redondo, there wasn't much of a problem with public access to the reconstituted creek because it would run along the street itself. But between Hardy and Clifton Street, there was no serious argument at the time for keeping that open to public access. Property owners adjoining it were too concerned about their security. Ultimately, it was gated at both ends, but a swale was created, which left the possibility open for those of us who were idealists to think that eventually it could be opened up to public access.

John English, *Oakland city planner, 1961-1978*

2005
TEMESCAL
PUMP STATION

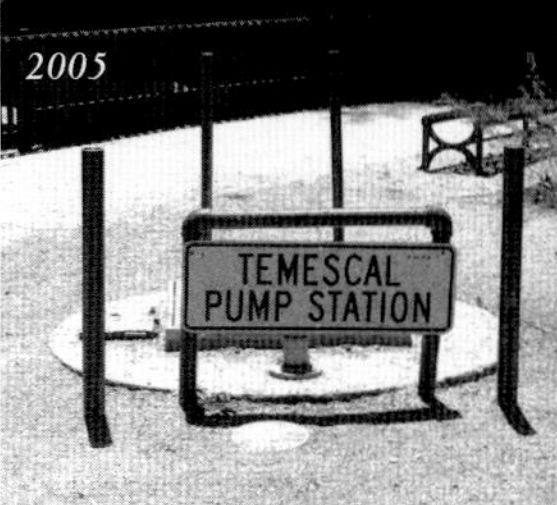

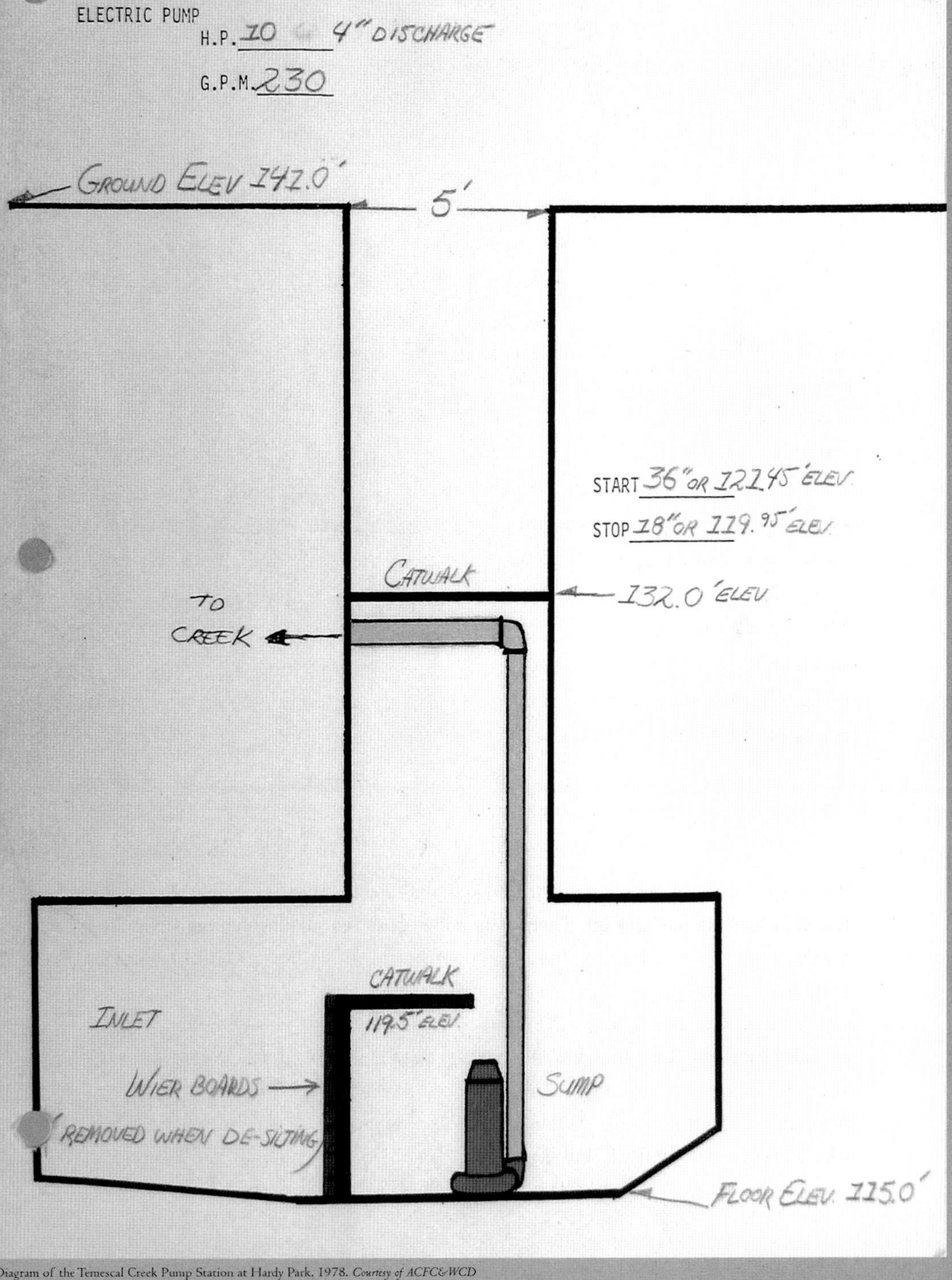
STATION
(TEMESCAL)
ELECTRIC PUMP
H.P. 10 4" DISCHARGE
G.P.M. 230
GROUND ELEV 142.0'
5'
START 36" OR 121.45' ELEV.
STOP 18" OR 119.95' ELEV.
CATWALK
132.0' ELEV.
TO CREEK
CATWALK
119.5' ELEV.
INLET
WIER BOARDS
(REMOVED WHEN DE-SILTING)
SUMP
FLOOR ELEV. 115.0'

Diagram of the Temescal Creek Pump Station at Hardy Park, 1978. *Courtesy of ACFC&WCD*

Maybe I'm directing this more to kids. But now that I'm reaching the other end of things, if I were living on Cavour, I wouldn't mind being able to go over and sit on a bench and look over a nice creek and hear some frogs. It wouldn't make my life any worse; it might add years to my life.

Dan: When I was driving back from Santa Cruz today, as I got off the freeway I saw this stretch of landscaping around the offramp where plum trees are in bloom. This year is a really good year for plum trees. The pink blossoms are more pronounced than I've seen in a long time. Below them were ceanothus, with all these blue blossoms. It really struck me. I tried to think what it is about flowers that people like. I mean, I think you can say that people generally like flowers. For me, a creek affects me in the same way. There's some kind of sustenance and connection that it provides. I think that's why they're important.

Peter: There is an intrinsic value to all living things, that maybe we can't describe, but that things like this offer. What happens to the kid who sees the frog? Does that change his life? Maybe. Or the old folks who walk down to the creek, hand in hand, and look in the water and see their reflection—and in water that doesn't turn off at five o'clock! There are a lot of parts of society that would benefit from having an open, urban creek. And it's being stolen from them—or it was stolen a long time ago. There's nothing like a creek to play in no matter how old you are! I don't think this is all that different from how we felt thirty years ago. ✦

Temescal Creek, off Thornhill Drive, 1997.

Caring for Our Creek Today

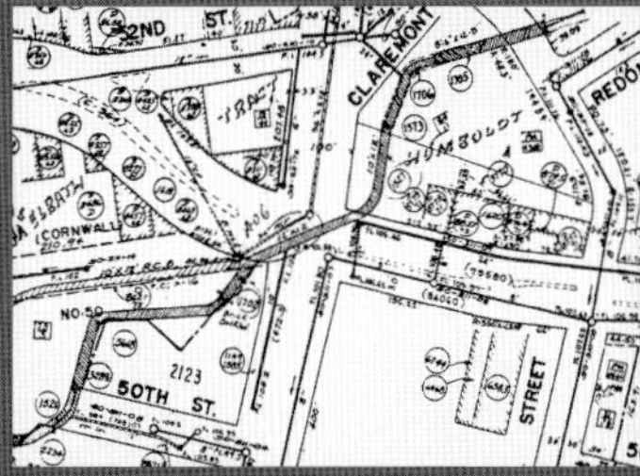

Storm drain diagram. *Courtesy of Public Works, City of Oakland*

Many people have a perception that storm drains are like toilets, somehow connected to a sewage treatment plant. But that's not how it is set up in the East Bay. On a rainy day, when you see water flowing down your driveway, or across a parking lot, or down the gutter of a road, that's actually an extension of the culverted creek. Water flows down a grade in the street, then typically through just a few hundred feet of pipe, and into the culverted creek. From there, it flows directly to the bay. If you put a chemical pesticide on your yard, or let your car drip oil on the road, or if you pour used oil down the storm drain—which hopefully people don't do anymore—that's the same as if you put any of those substances in a small creek in the woods.

✦ Using the principles of Integrated Pest Management (IPM), we can avoid using substances like chemical fertilizers and pesticides, which are hazardous to all forms of life, especially to microorganisms and insects and invertebrates—the small crawly creatures that are the basis of the food chain. We can avoid chemical fertilizers by using compost and organic fertilizers, which are widely available. We can avoid the use of pesticides. Pest problems can be solved by mechanical means, like clipping off affected branches or just putting up with a certain amount of fruit or flowers that are spoiled by whatever insect is bothering them. There are natural products for controlling things like ants. Then there's the matter of timing: if you feel you have to use a pesticide, apply it only when it's not going to rain so that it has time to soak in, do its job, and decompose before something comes to wash it into the storm drain.

✦ When we fertilize our lawns and water them to the point where water is pouring out of the yard and into the street, then we're directly washing the fertilizer into the creek. The solution is simply to cut down on the amount of water used. It will save you money, cut down on water waste, and also help your lawn not succumb to fungus. If you use an irrigation system, make sure that it is working properly and not leaking excessively or being overused. Also, consider landscaping with native plants that require less or no water and fertilizer.

✦ If your car has an oil leak, get it serviced so that it doesn't drip out oil onto the road. Also, dispose of oil, paint, and household chemicals properly.

✦ Street sweeping, inconvenient perhaps and irritating with the potential bi-monthly expense of parking tickets, is an important and effective way to reduce the amount of toxic material in the dust on the road and to reduce the amount of organic matter such as leaves flowing into the creek and the bay. Cooperating with the street sweeping program, and being sure to remember to move your car, also saves you money and helps have cleaner streets.

✦ Friends of Temescal Creek has monthly water testing days and quarterly series of tests to check bacteria levels. Currently we're collecting samples at Lake Temescal and the Rockridge-Temescal Greenbelt, where people actually can play in the creek water. We are hoping to carry out a watershed-wide testing program, and we welcome people to help collect water samples.

Bruce Douglas

Temescal Creek Water Quality

In April 2003 we had a "founding meeting" of a small group of people interested in water quality monitoring. I volunteered to start bacteriological testing on the creek below Lake Temescal. So I drove around, walked, rode my bike, and found four sites that were easy to get to: St. Albert's Priory, on Birch Court; Oakvale Road, off Claremont, on the Harwood Creek tributary to the main creek; Frog Park at the pump; and the open culvert that runs through the Bay Street Mall in Emeryville. I did three sequences that first year. Each involved taking a sample from the sites once a week for five weeks in a row, and delivering them to the Richmond Field Station where the EPA ran the tests.

The results were basically comparable to other East Bay creeks. There's a baseline of coliform that's always present in the creeks, from animals and plants. But it's the presence of *E. coli* that shows fecal contamination. There's a certain range above which it's dangerous for human contact. But it doesn't look like there's much contamination in Temescal Creek, although it's variable, and occasionally in the summer, because of the low flow, the count gets higher. This isn't a problem as long as people know that they shouldn't drink the water, and to wash their hands after playing in it and before eating.

There are some immediate benefits to this work. A few years back, there was raw sewage leaking into the creek higher upstream, so people who had the creek flowing through their yards were at risk for illness. We found out about this through testing and alerted the city so that the problem was fixed.

Doing this kind of work also helps Temescal Creek because it helps me. Knowing what's in the water is one step on a path toward becoming completely part of my watershed. Through understanding what is in the creek water, I can recognize the interdependence of everything. And it has a kind of feedback in my behavior: "Oh well, then, I won't wash my car in the street anymore."

Where people live for generations, the land becomes sacred. That's an integral part of being human and living in a place. But our land has lost its legends and myths. Perhaps what we're doing with Temescal Creek, our ways of caring for it, is the very beginning of some movement towards re-mythologizing the land.

Joan Marie Wood
Volunteer, Friends of
Temescal Creek

Joan Marie Wood, collecting a water sample from Temescal Creek, St. Albert's Priory, February 2006.

Aerial photo, showing stretch of Temescal Creek (the dark band of trees) from the Grove-Shafter Freeway to San Pablo Avenue, 1970. *Courtesy of the ACFC&WCD*

There's a tremendous need for connection between those of us who live here and those who live further down toward the bay. As you go from the hills to the bay, it seems that there is more and more concrete, that more and more of the land has been paved over. The lack of places for there to be birds and insects and water is a terrible lack in our lives. We really suffer from this, even though it's hard to quantify. That awareness is something that could be shared on a very basic, human level, no matter what our income differences are. It's worth stretching oneself to make those connections, because it can be so beneficial—to pull together people who have a common interest because they're all affected by living in the same watershed.

Joan Marie Wood
Volunteer, Friends of
Temescal Creek

Temescal Creek clean-up day, Rockridge-Temescal Greenbelt, April 2005.

Acknowledgments

Like any community effort, this book would not have been possible without the support of many individuals and organizations. First and foremost, for the book's very heart and soul, I thank those who spent hours, uninhibited by the tape recorder, generously sharing their memories: Frederick Brooks, Theresa Brooks, Dan deGrassi, Bruce Douglas, John English, Marian Gatti, Sewall Glinternick, Aldo Guidotti, Madison Harvey, Donald Hausler, Peter Heylin, Gladys M. Jordan, Raymond Mellana, Bill Martino, Donald Olsen, Carol Pulcifer, Tony Rago, Ray Raineri, Paul Smith, Morrie Turner, and Joan Marie Wood.

Searching for and finding the documents that augment the interviews was a rewarding process in and of itself. Making it all the more pleasurable was working with the many local institutions and collectors who graciously made their collections available to me. For their kindness, and expertise, I thank the African American Museum and Library at Oakland, Alameda County Flood Control and Water Conservation District, Ronald Avanzino, The Bancroft Library, Caltrans Photography Department–District 4, Dan deGrassi, Alphonse and Annette Durieux, the Ecology Center, John Harder, Hills Newspaper Group, Library of Congress, Raymond Mellana, Oakland Cultural Heritage Survey, Oakland History Room at the Oakland Public Library, Oakland Museum of California, Ray Raineri, Paul Smith, Eileen Suzio, and the Ted Wurm Collection.

Numerous people, out of personal friendship or in ways that went beyond their professional duty, helped move this project along: Gloria Aquiar (Alameda County Flood Control and Water Conservation District Map Library), Annalee Allen, Martha Bergmann (Oakland History Room), Betty Brown (Hills Newspaper Group), Dennis Brown, Steve Costa, Sylvia Dewitt (Caltrans Photography Department – District 4), Jennifer Dowling, Dennis Evanosky, John Evans (Diesel Books), John Fenstermacher (Alameda County Flood Control and Water Conservation District), Tom Gerstel (Thunder Road Treatment Center), Patrizia Guccione (Alameda Countywide Clean Water Program), Jackie Hoeppner-Freitas, Donald Hausler, Frances Heath (East Bay Regional Park District), Dick Jenevein, Rena Keough (Alameda County Flood Control and Water Conservation District Map Library), Steve Lavoie (Oakland History Room), Gail Lombardi (Oakland Cultural Heritage Survey), Pamela Magnuson-Peddle, Betty Marvin (Oakland Cultural Heritage Survey), Shannon McQueen (African American Museum and Library at Oakland), Johnette Jones Morton (Studio One Art Center),

Rick Moss (African American Museum and Library at Oakland), Tom Panas (El Cerrito Historical Society), Jennifer Pearson, Allison Reid (Diesel Books), Ray Raineri, Kathy Rogers (Con Le Nostre Mani exhibit), G. Mac Sebree, Robert O. Self, Steve Smith, Di Starr, Joan Suzio, Nelia White, and Betty Wurm.

I also relied upon several friends and colleagues to read portions of this book. While the responsibility for its content and design is mine alone, the book benefited significantly from their careful scrutiny, expert editorial eye, and excellent suggestions. For this, I am indebted to Beth Blackman, Martha Bergmann, Anna Jing Brown, Jennifer Dowling, Kathy Geritz, Carla Koop, Pamela Magnuson-Peddle, Ray Raineri, Alyse Smith, Steve Smith, and Nelia White.

My deepest appreciation is reserved for my wife, Kathy Geritz, whose belief in the project and steady encouragement made it possible for me to keep putting one foot in front of the other.

Funding for this book was provided by the Oakland City Council and the City of Oakland's Cultural Funding Program, in the form of an Individual Artist Grant; and from the Alameda Countywide Clean Water Program, which awarded the project a Stewardship Grant. This book would not exist had it not been for their generous financial support.

Teen mobile-making workshop, Studio One, 1954.
Courtesy of the Oakland History Room

Community Resources

Local History Resources

The Bancroft Library. A major center for research at the University of California, consisting of a non-circulating collection of books, manuscripts, pictures, maps, and other materials. UC Berkeley, CA 94720; 510/642-6481; www.bancroft.berkeley.edu

Building Department, City of Oakland. Building permits for post-1905 buildings are available on microfiche. 250 Frank Ogawa Plaza, 2nd floor, Oakland, CA 94612; 510/238-3443

Landmarks Preservation Advisory Board. The City of Oakland's program for officially designating select Landmarks and Preservation Districts, and Potential Designated Historic Properties. 250 Frank Ogawa Plaza, Third Floor, Oakland, CA 94612; 510/238-2978; www.oaklandnet.com/government/ceda/revised/planningzoning/HistoricPreservation

Oakland Cultural Heritage Survey. A program of the city's Planning and Zoning Division that surveys, researches, and maintains an extensive library of information on historic properties and districts in Oakland. 250 Frank Ogawa Plaza, Third Floor, Oakland, CA 94612; 510/238-6879

Oakland Heritage Alliance. A non-profit membership organization working to protect, preserve, and revitalize Oakland's architectural, historic, cultural, and natural resources through publications, education, and direct action. 446-17th St., Suite 301, Oakland, CA 94612; 510/763-9218; www.oaklandheritage.org

Oakland History Room, Oakland Public Library. A center and library for the study of the history and ongoing development of the San Francisco Bay Area, with a special emphasis on Oakland and the East Bay. 125-14th St., Oakland, CA 94612; 510/238-3222

Oakland Museum of California. The museum's website offers many online resources, including thousands of images relating to California. 1000 Oak St., Oakland, CA 94607; 510/238-2200; www.museumca.org/global/resources.html

Studio One

Department of Parks and Recreation, City of Oakland. Offers a wide range of services, activities, and programs to Oakland citizens and visitors. 510/238-4245; www.oaklandnet.com/parks

Friends of Studio One. A non-profit organization supporting the City of Oakland's historic Studio One Art Center at 365-45th St. and its programs. 510/420-5852; www.friendsofstudioone.org

Studio One Art Center. A city-run studio arts facility operating since 1949, where adults and children study, create, and share art in a supportive environment. 365-45th St., Oakland, CA 94609; 510/597-5027; www.oaklandnet.com/parks/facilities/rc_studioone.asp

Sacramento Northern Railway

Bay Area Rails. A website created by Montclair resident Sam Lewit, featuring a photo gallery and interactive maps on historic Bay Area railroads, including the Sacramento Northern Railway. www.bayarearailfan.org

Catenary Video Productions. A major source for videos on vintage railroads, produced from rare archival footage. P.O. Box 10577, Oakland, CA 94610. 800/343-5540; www.catenaryvideo.com

Dan Webb Books. Specializing in aviation, military, and railroad books. 15 Grand Ave., Oakland, CA 94612; 510/444-4572; www.danwebbbooks.com

Sacramento Northern On-line. A website featuring extensive information, images (including of the rail yard at 40th and Shafter), a bibliography of books and articles, and links on the subject of the Sacramento Northern Railway. www.people.virginia.edu

Western Railway Museum. A living history museum, library, and archives focusing on streetcars and interurban electric trains from California and the western U.S. 5848 State Hwy. 12, Suisun, CA 94585; 707/374-2978; www.wrm.org

Grove-Shafter Freeway

Bay Area Rapid Transit website. History and facts, including a full chronology, about BART's development, funding, and construction. www.bart.gov/about/history/history_3.asp

Caltrans Library. Located in Sacramento on N between 11th and 12th, next to the State Capitol, the library is open to the public by appointment only. 916/654-4601; www.dot.ca.gov/hq/esc/CHPC/historylinks.html

Caltrans, District 4, Photography Department. A source of historic and recent photos (digital and film), including aerials, of Bay Area Caltrans projects. 111 Grand Ave., Room 12-325, Oakland, CA 94612; 510/286-6179; www.dot.ca.gov/dist4/photography/

California Highways. A website providing information on California highways and their history. www.cahighways.org

East Bay Negro Historical Society

African American Museum and Library at Oakland. A reference library, archives, and museum dedicated to the history and culture of African Americans in California and the West. 659-14th St., Oakland, CA 94612; 510/637-0200; www.oaklandlibrary.org/AAMLO/collection.html

Oakland Citizens Committee for Urban Renewal. A public interest advocacy organization addressing the urban and political development of the City of Oakland. 1330 Broadway, Suite 1030, Oakland, CA 94612; 510/839-2440. www.eastmont.net/occur.htm

Temescal Creek

Alameda Countywide Clean Water Program. A consortium of local agencies working to prevent stormwater pollution and restore the health of local watersheds, creeks, and the San Francisco Bay. ACCWP funds projects that contain a stormwater pollution prevention message. 510/670-5543; www.cleanwaterprogram.org

Alameda County Flood Control and Water Conservation District, Map Library. Maps, plans, reports, and other documents relating to Alameda County's flood control projects. 399 Elmhust St., Room 240, Hayward, CA 94544; 510/670-5559

East Bay Watershed Center. Housed at Merritt College, the Center facilitates local watershed stewardship and management by citizen groups, schools, planners, land owners, businesses, and elected officials. 12500 Campus Dr., Oakland, CA 94619; 510/434-3840; www.merritt.edu/~envst/watershed.html

Ecology Center. A non-profit, membership organization offering a wide array of local and regional environmental services, programs, and publications. 2530 San Pablo Ave., Berkeley 94702; 510/548-2220; www.ecologycenter.org

Friends of Temescal Creek. A community organization providing education, policy analysis, water quality sampling, and other activities to help protect Temescal Creek and its watershed. 510/434-3840; www.thewatershedproject.org/temescal

Our Water, Our World Partnership Program. Provides information on alternatives to using pesticides. www.ourwaterourworld.org

Save the Bay. A non-profit membership organization providing educational and outreach activities to help protect and restore San Francisco Bay. 510/452-9261; www.savesfbay.org

The Watershed Project. Offers workshops for home gardeners, educators and the general public about local creeks, wetlands, and watersheds, and provides support for creek protection groups. 510/665-3546; www.thewatershedproject.org

Urban Creeks Council of California. A statewide non-profit organization working to preserve, protect, and restore urban streams and their riparian habitat. 1250 Addison St., #107C, Berkeley, CA 94702. 510/540-6669; www.urbancreeks.org

Watershed Improvement Program, City of Oakland Public Works Agency. Provides information on creek stewardship, creek restoration projects, and stormwater pollution prevention in Oakland, and on the City's Creek Protection Ordinance. Report illegal dumping in or near creeks. 250 Frank H. Ogawa Plaza, Suite 5301, Oakland, CA 94612; 510/238-6600; www.oaklandpw.com/creeks/index.htm

Water Resource Center Archives. A library of contemporary and historic materials on all aspects of water resources. 410 O'Brien Hall, UC Berkeley, Berkeley, CA 94720; 510/642-2666; www.lib.berkeley.edu/WRCA

Sources

Studio One

Claremont Press, November 6, 1953; July 8, 1960.
English, John, draft of application to list Studio One on the National Register of Historic Places, 2005.
Grant Deed from Recreation Center Committee of the North Oakland Area Council, a non-profit corporation, to the City of Oakland, a municipal corporation, January 26, 1948.
Guidotti, Aldo P., personal interview, August 13, 2004.
Montclarion, June 5, 1947; October 2, 1947.
Oakland Heritage Alliance News, Summer 1995.
Oakland Post-Enquirer, April 18, 1947; June 27, 1947; April 12, 1949; May 13, 1949.
Oakland Telegraph, October 30, 1959.
Oakland Tribune, June 27, 1947; June 29, 1947; August 22, 1947; August 24, 1947; September 24, 1947; August 26, 1948; September 17, 1949; September 19, 1949; May 4, 1952; January 3, 1954; June 10, 1964; March 24, 1965; March 26, 1969.
Pulcifer, Zelma Carol, personal interview, February 28, 2005.
Sanborn Insurance Map (Vol. 3), circa 1932.
"Studio One Art Center—A Brief Story" (booklet), by Terry Hatcher and Carol Pulcifer, 1989.

Sacramento Northern Railway

Claremont Press, August 19, 1960; May 29, 1975; August 7, 1975.
Certificate of Occupancy, 4001-05-07 Webster St. and 424-40th St., Oakland, Calif., December 4, 1961, Building Department, City of Oakland.
City of Oakland, official records, June 26, 1911.
Contra Costa Gazette, May 5, 1911.
Demolition permit to wreck office and baggage room, northwest corner of Shafter and 40th St., Oakland, Calif., April 22, 1957, Building Department, City of Oakland.
Electric Interurban Railways in America, George W. Hilton and John F. Due, Stanford University Press, 1960.
Electric Journal, 1913.
Electric Railways Around San Francisco Bay, Volume Two, Compiled by Donald Duke, Golden West Books, San Marino, Calif., 2000.
English, John, application to list Studio One on the National Register of Historic Places, 2005.
"History of the Physical Development of the City of Oakland: The Formative Years, 1850-1930," by John Beatty Dykstra, 1967, masters thesis, University of California, Berkeley.
Interurbans Special 9: Sacramento Northern, Ira L. Swett, ed., 1950.
Interurbans Special 26: Sacramento Northern, Ira L. Swett, ed., 1963.
Hausler, Donald, personal interview, May 23, 2005.
Lafayette Sun, August 6, 1954; September 10, 1954.
Montclarion, April 17, 1947; July 17, 1947; July 31, 1947; July 24, 1947; July 31, 1947; September 25, 1947; October 16, 1947; November 13, 1947; November 20, 1947; June 17, 1948; July 1, 1948; August 5, 1948; August 12, 1948; July 1, 1948; November 17, 1971; October 4, 1994.
Montclarion Then and Now, April 1998.
Oakland Enquirer, January 5, 1911; June 8, 1911; October 21, 1911.

Oakland Post-Enquirer, July 11, 1947.
Oakland Telegraph, August 7, 1965.
Oakland This Week (a *Montclarion* publication), May 18, 1984.
Oakland Tribune, June 18, 1940; September 24, 1947; March 11, 1951; February 10, 1957; February 26, 1957; March 1, 1957; April 25, 1957; May 24, 1957; December 1, 1957; April 7, 1963; June 16, 1968; June 7, 1972.
Olsen, Don, personal interview, November 2, 2004.
Raineri, Raymond, personal interview, June 9, 2005.
Realty Syndicate Financial Statement, September 29, 1900.
Sanborn Insurance Maps, 1911, updated 1932; circa 1951; circa 1967.
San Francisco Examiner, March 1, 1957.
Smith, Paul D., personal interview, November 16, 2004.

Grove-Shafter Freeway

American Babylon: Race and the Struggle for Postwar Oakland, by Robert O. Self, Princeton University Press, Princeton, New Jersey, 2003.
California Highway Transportation Agency, correspondence: memorandum from R. A. Hayler, Division of Highways–District IV, to J. P. Sinclair, January 29, 1964.
City of Oakland, correspondence: letter from Corwin R. Mocine, City Planning Engineer, to Sewall Glinternick, Editor and Publisher, *Claremont Press,* November 5, 1956; letter from John A, Morin, Superintendent of Streets, to B. W. Booker, Assistant State Highway Engineer, December 19, 1957.
Claremont Press, January 29, 1960; July 8, 1960; May 3, 1968.
Glinternick, Sewall, personal interview, February 19, 2005.
Guidotti, Aldo P., personal interview, August 13, 2004.
Hausler, Donald, personal interview, May 23, 2005.
Index to California Highways and Public Works, 1937-1967, Volume I, California Department of Transportation, 1997. www.dot.ca.gov.
Mellana, Raymond E. personal interview, August 10, 2004.
Montclarion, April 10, 1984.
Oakland Telegraph, October 30, 1959.
Oakland Tribune, July 18, 1958; February 27, 1959; September 22, 1960; May 28, 1961; April 18, 1963; October 24, 1963; January 9, 1964; February 23, 1964; March 2, 1964; March 5, 1964; April 26, 1966; June 3, 1966; July 28, 1966; August 7, 1966; January 15, 1967; April 6, 1967; January 15, 1969; July 22, 1969; July 24, 1969; September 23, 1969; December 15, 1969; November 8, 1970; July 20, 1971; January 21, 1973; December 1, 1986; August 8, 2004.
Raineri, Raymond, personal interview, June 9, 2005.
"Report and Findings of Hearing Commissioners of the California Highway Commission re Freeway Location IV-Ala,C.C-226,75-Oak,A (Grove-Shafter Freeway)," May 22, 1958.
Sanborn Insurance Maps, updated 1932; circa 1951; circa 1967.
San Francisco Examiner, March 2, 1964; March 31, 1967; April 9, 1973.

East Bay Negro Historical Society

"A Brief History of the Northern California Center for African American History and Life" (unpublished notes), by Gladys Meriwether Jordan, 1999.
A Fine Old Conflict, by Jessica Mitford, Alfred A. Knopf, New York, 1977.

American Babylon: Race and the Struggle for Postwar Oakland, by Robert O. Self, Princeton University Press, Princeton, New Jersey, 2003.

"Blacks in Oakland: 1852-1987" (unpublished paper), by Donald Hausler, 1987.

Brooks, Theresa and Frederick, personal interview, February 17, 2005.

Class Aspects of Residential Development and Choice in the Oakland Black Community, by William Henry Brown, Jr., 1970. Ph.D. dissertation (Geography), University of California, Berkeley.

East Bay Negro Historical Society, misc. documents: Quarter-Annual Report, September 27, 1974; flyer, 1982; brochure (undated); newsletter, Vol. I, No. I, January-February 1986.

From the Archives, published by the Northern California Center for Afro-American History and Life, Spring 1991; Winter 1991.

Glinternick, Sewall, personal interview, February 19, 2005.

Harvey, Madison, personal interview, May 17, 2005.

Hausler, Donald, personal interview, May 23, 2005.

Jordan, Gladys Meriwether, personal interview, August 12, 2004, and September 14, 2004.

Library of Congress, Prints & Photographs Online Catalog. www.loc.gov/rr/print/catalog.html

Montclarion, September 29, 1971.

Negro Trail Blazers of California, The, by Delilah L. Beasley, 1919.

"Neighborhood Profiles: North Oakland," Oakland Citizens Committee for Urban Renewal, circa 1997.

Northern California Center for Afro-American History & Life, newsletter, Fall 1993.

No There There: Race, Class, and Political Community in Oakland, by Chris Rhomberg, University of California Press, 2004.

Oakland Heritage Alliance News, Winter, 1986; Summer 1986.

Oakland Tribune, February 7, 1971; April 18, 1971; August 8, 1971; February 11, 1973; February, 12, 1973; March 27, 1976; July 11, 1977; July 14, 1985; August 30, 2000; September 20, 2001; August 31, 2004; February 25, 2005.

Parallel Communities: African Americans in California's East Bay, 1850-1963, by Delores Nason McBroome Garland Publishing, Inc., New York and London, 1993.

Pulcifer, Zelma Carol, personal interview, February 28, 2005.

Raineri, Raymond, personal interview, June 9, 2005.

San Francisco Chronicle, January 31, 1986; January 19, 2004.

Turner, Morris, personal interview, January 13, 2005.

Visions Toward Tomorrow: The History of the East Bay Afro-American Community, 1852-1977, by Lawrence P. Crouchette, Lonnie G. Bunch, III, Martha Kendall Winnacker, 1989, Northern California Center for Afro-American History and Life, Oakland, Calif.

United States Census Bureau, Statistic for Census Tracts, 1940–2000.

Temescal Creek

Building permit to build Safeway, 5354 Claremont Ave., Oakland, Calif., September 21, 1960; Certificate of Occupancy, August 28, 1961, Building Department, City of Oakland.

"Appraisal Report, Reach 3, Temescal Creek," Urban Property Research Company, March 1972.

Creek Speak, March/April 1990.

County of Alameda, correspondence: letter from Herbert G. Crowle, Director of Public Works to J. P. Sinclair, Assistant State Highway Engineer, June 14, 1963; letter from Paul E. Lanferman, Engineer-Manager, Alameda County Flood Control and Water Conservation District to Mr. and Mrs. Willie Thomas, June 28, 1974; letter from Paul E. Lanferman, Engineer-Manager, Alameda County Flood Control and Water Conservation District to Jon Fox, *Oakland Tribune,* June 28, 1974; letter from Cliff Pletschet, *Oakland Tribune* to Herbert G. Crowle, Director of Public Works, Alameda County, August

14, 1974; inter-office communication from Paul E. Lanferman, Engineer-Manager, Alameda County Flood Control and Water Conservation District to Herbert G. Crowle, Director of Public Works, Alameda County, August 22, 1974; letter from Paul E. Lanferman, Engineer-Manager, Alameda County Flood Control and Water Conservation District to Cliff Pletschet, *Oakland Tribune,* August 27, 1974; inter-department communication from Paul E. Lanferman, Engineer-Manager, Alameda County Flood Control and Water Conservation District to Alameda County Supervisor Thomas H. Bates, October 8, 1975.

deGrassi, Dan, personal interview, February 19, 2005.

Douglas, L. Bruce, personal interviews, December 6 and December 8, 2004.

Ecology Center Newsletter, March 1971; April 1971; May 1971; August 1971; March 1973.

"Engineering Report–Final Draft, Temescal Creek Improvements, Line A, Zone 12 for ACFC&WCD," Walter Long & Associates, March 15, 1977.

English, John, personal interview, April 18, 2005.

Environmental Impact Statement, "The Improvement of a Portion of Line A – Temescal Creek, from San Pablo Avenue to Adeline Street and from the vicinity of Telegraph Avenue to the Vicinity of Hardy Street in Oakland and Emeryville, California." Bissell & Karn, Inc., San Leandro, California, February 1972.

Gatti, Marian L., personal interview, November 17, 2004.

Guidotti, Aldo P., personal interview, August 13, 2004.

Heylin, Peter, personal interview, February 19, 2005.

Martino, Bill, personal interview, November 18, 2004.

North Oakland District Community Council Newsletter, March 1981; January 1982; January 1983.

Oakland Tribune, May 19, 1971.

Petition to culvert Temescal Creek from Market to Grove, June 11, 1974.

"Questionnaire, Temescal Creek Residents," Department of Landscape Architecture, UC Berkeley, Winter 1971.

"Report on Improvement of Temescal Creek from Grove Street to Vicinity of Ivanhoe Road, Zone No. 12 Project," Alameda County Flood Control and Water Conservation District, October 1964.

Sanborn Insurance Maps, 1911, updated 1932; circa 1951; circa 1967.

Temescal Pump Station Data, Alameda County Public Works Agency, April 1978.

Temescal Album: History of a Neighborhood, Shared Ground, 1998.

"Urban Park Over Troubled Waters: Assessing Urban Park Values from Community Meetings," by Nelia White, 1999. A course paper in Geography, San Francisco State University.

Where We Live: Stories from Temescal, video, Shared Ground, 1998.

Wood, Joan Marie, personal interview, April 15, 2005.

Yodler, Sierra Club Bay Chapter, March 1972.

Shattuck and Telegraph Avenue "gore" at 45th Street, (looking north), Original Kasper's Hotdogs at center, 1948. *Courtesy of the Oakland History Room*

Index: Streets and Highways

52nd Street overpass, 2005.

Index: General

T

U

V

W

Telegraph and Claremont (looking south), circa 1967. *Courtesy of the Oakland Cultural Heritage Survey*

Temescal Creek, near Adeline and 47th Street, 1970. *Courtesy of Alameda County Flood Control & Water Conservation District*

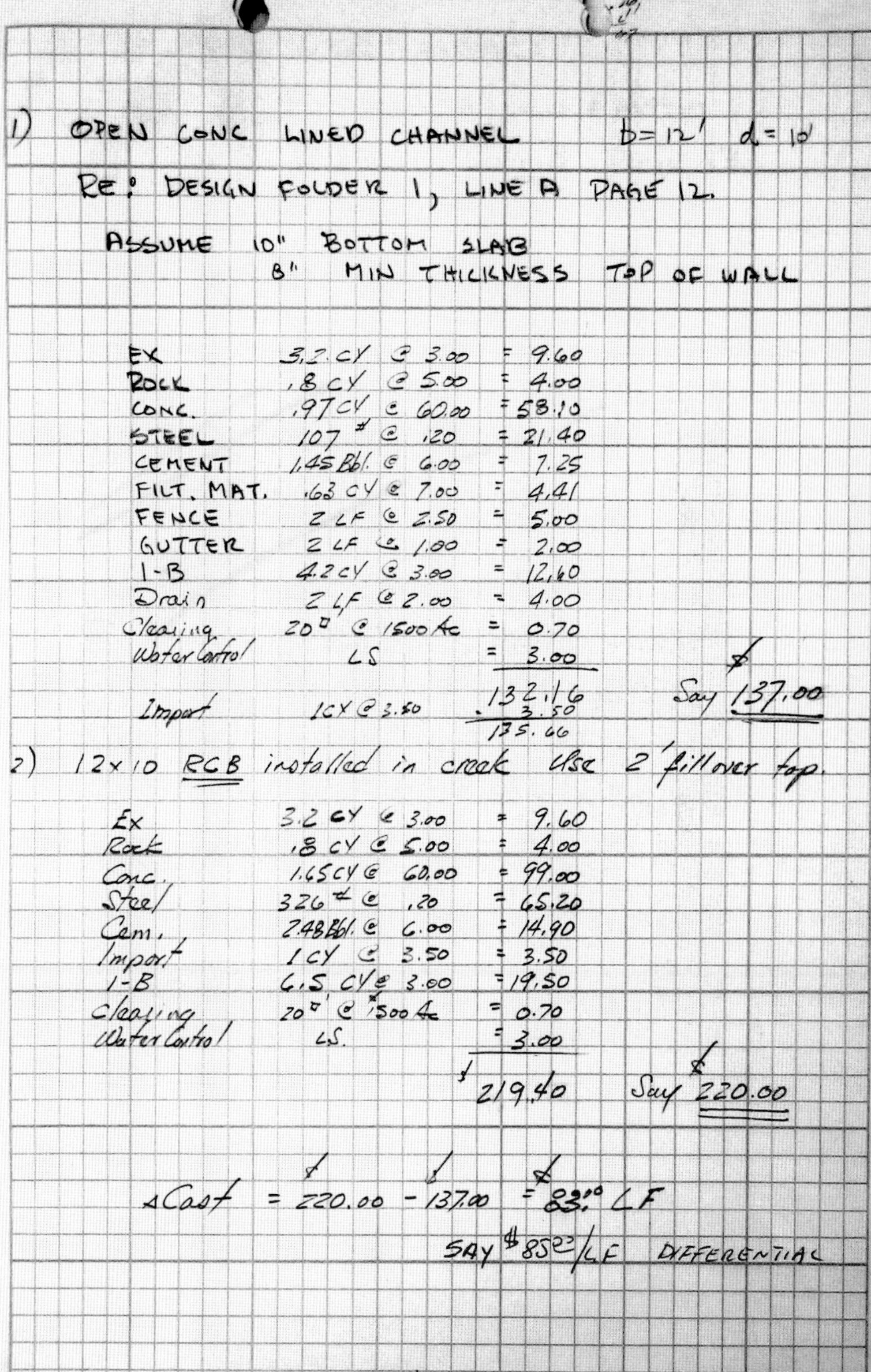

1) OPEN CONC LINED CHANNEL b = 12' d = 10'

RE: DESIGN FOLDER 1, LINE A PAGE 12.

ASSUME 10" BOTTOM SLAB
8" MIN THICKNESS TOP OF WALL

EX	3.2 CY @ 3.00	= 9.60	
ROCK	.8 CY @ 5.00	= 4.00	
CONC.	.97 CY @ 60.00	= 58.10	
STEEL	107 # @ .20	= 21.40	
CEMENT	1.45 Bbl. @ 6.00	= 7.25	
FILT. MAT.	.63 CY @ 7.00	= 4.41	
FENCE	2 LF @ 2.50	= 5.00	
GUTTER	2 LF @ 1.00	= 2.00	
I-B	4.2 CY @ 3.00	= 12.60	
Drain	2 LF @ 2.00	= 4.00	
Clearing	20 □ @ 1500 Ac	= 0.70	
Water Control	LS	= 3.00	
		132.16	
Import	1 CY @ 3.50	3.50	
		135.66	Say $ 137.00

2) 12 x 10 RCB installed in creek Use 2' fill over top.

Ex	3.2 CY @ 3.00	= 9.60	
Rock	.8 CY @ 5.00	= 4.00	
Conc.	1.65 CY @ 60.00	= 99.00	
Steel	326 # @ .20	= 65.20	
Cem.	2.48 Bbl. @ 6.00	= 14.90	
Import	1 CY @ 3.50	= 3.50	
I-B	6.5 CY @ 3.00	= 19.50	
Clearing	20 □ @ 1500 Ac	= 0.70	
Water Control	LS.	= 3.00	
		$ 219.40	Say $ 220.00

Δ Cost = $ 220.00 − $ 137.00 = $ 83.00 LF

SAY $85.00/LF DIFFERENTIAL

Materials estimate, Temescal Creek culvert, 1964. *Courtesy of Alameda County Flood Control & Water Conservation District*

Notes

MOTIVE POWER AND CAR DEPARTMENT
AGREEMENT BETWEEN
THE
SACRAMENTO NORTHERN RAILWAY
AND
SYSTEM FEDERATION No. 158
RAILWAY EMPLOYES DEPARTMENT
AMERICAN FEDERATION OF LABOR
MECHANICAL SECTION THEREOF

EFFECTIVE JULY 1, 1937

Courtesy of Ronald Avanzino

For thirty years JEFF NORMAN has been using images and text to explore our understanding of our everyday environments. As a community artist, he has completed several interdisciplinary projects that examine the connections between Temescal's past and present. He has made his home in Temescal since 1984.

Founded in 1997, SHARED GROUND is a community arts organization dedicated to enhancing the cultural and ecological vitality of the Temescal neighborhood of Oakland, California, and neighborhoods in general. Values underlying the projects of SHARED GROUND include sustainability, love of place, strengthening local identity, historic preservation, diversity, collaboration, and activism.

For more information about SHARED GROUND's projects and publications:

SHARED GROUND
477 Rich Street, Oakland, California 94609
(510) 653-7190
SharedGround@california.com
www.sharedground.org

Photo of Jeff Norman, above: Kathy Geritz

Street map of North Oakland (detail), 2005.